T0171357

Unveiled

52 Weekly Devotions for Encountering God

BERT LEWIS

And we all, with unveiled face, beholding the glory of the Lord, are being transformed into the same image from one degree of glory to another. For this comes from the Lord who is the Spirit

2 Corinthians 3:18

WESTBOW
PRESS
A DIVISION OF THOMAS NELSON

WestBow Press books may be ordered through booksellers or by contacting:

WestBow Press
A Division of Thomas Nelson
1663 Liberty Drive
Bloomington, IN 47403
www.westbowpress.com
1-(866) 928-1240

ISBN: 978-1-4497-9332-6 (sc)
ISBN: 978-1-4497-9333-3 (hc)
ISBN: 978-1-4497-9331-9 (e)

Library of Congress Control Number: 2013907499

Printed in the United States of America.

WestBow Press rev. date: 05/22/2013

Table of Contents

Acknowledgments

To Karen, Kristin, and Logan: thank you for letting me share this with you and for allowing me to ask over and over, "Does this sound okay?" Thanks for helping me find the right words. I love you more than you know! To my friends and family who have allowed me to share portions of *Unveiled* with you, thank you for your encouragement, prayers, and suggestions along the way. To Hunter Street Baptist Church for teaching sound biblical doctrine for which there is no substitute. I know there are many wonderful churches, but I thank God for mine because it's the one where He has chosen to love, teach, and encourage me. Mostly, I thank God for giving His Son, Jesus Christ, for me, a sinner. Thank you, God, for your saving grace and your continuing daily grace! Help me live a life worthy of that grace.

Foreword

I am convinced no one can grow and develop into a mature follower of Christ without a consistent and thoughtful time of private devotions. That is why I am delighted to recommend this volume and its unique approach to assisting the believer in encountering God through His Word each day.

Let me say a word about Bert Lewis. It has been my joy to be both Bert's friend and pastor since 2003. He is a loving husband and father, a successful businessman, a faithful Bible teacher, and a man after God's own heart. He knows God and has learned to meet face to face and heart to heart with his heavenly Father. As Bert has done this, he has become more and more like Christ.

He has written this devotional to assist believers to regularly behold and contemplate the glory of Christ so they may be transformed into His image. When we behold Christ—when we fix our attention, the eyes of our faith on Him—we are transformed. According to Romans 8:29, this is the purpose for which God chose us in the beginning: "For those whom he foreknew he also predestined to be conformed to the image of his Son." It is toward this purpose that God works everything together.

So, how do we behold Him? Well, [the way] we behold anything we can't see with our eyes. How do you focus on knowing your husband or wife (which you could do even if you were blind)? How do you focus on goals and plans for your business? How do you focus on anything you care about? You give attention to it. You seek to know all you can about it. You spend time on it. You concentrate and think and mull it over in your mind in between everything else.

And the same is true of beholding the glory of Christ Jesus. It takes time and attention. It demands that we put other things aside. Specifically, James says we look in the mirror of His Word.

I believe *Unveiled* is a wonderful tool that the Spirit of God will use to help you to focus your mind's attention and your heart's affection on Christ so you will treasure Him above all things. And as that happens, there will be genuine transformation of your life from the inside out.

Soli Deo Gloria (Glory to God alone),

Buddy

Buddy Gray, Pastor

Hunter Street Baptist Church

Preface

The Purpose of Unveiled

We search for answers in many different ways, using many different resources. It is human nature to want to know the answer to life's most important questions. Unfortunately, we are at times misled as to where those answers can be found. Too often we look to the world for an answer, and the world may give us one, but rarely is it the correct one. The answers to life's most important questions are found in the Scriptures. We just have to make the decision to diligently search for God's will in the Scriptures and then listen, as His answers are always right. There is a stark contrast between God and man, and a primary purpose of *Unveiled* is to show us that difference. To understand how great and loving God is we first need to understand who we are before Him. We are sinners saved by grace, designed and created by God to bring Him glory. I hope this becomes apparent as you encounter these pages. I hope you see Jesus Christ magnified.

The inspiration for these passages came from a variety of situations. It could have been through personal Bible reading, study in preparation for a Sunday school lesson, or a passage or point referenced in a sermon preached. At other times, it was hearing a prayer, remembering a testimony, and even family circumstances or personal experiences that caused me to recall or search out a particular verse of Scripture. Ultimately, though, the Holy Spirit was the catalyst for these verses. Over a period of time, the Lord put these fifty-two verses on my heart; first for the verse to change me and then for me to share them with you.

Why a Weekly Devotional and Suggestions for Its Use

Sometimes when we eat, we prefer a small taste before really digging in, and that's okay. In *Unveiled*, there are fifty-two devotions for your reading that will stir your heart and mind, and passages of Scripture have been provided for subsequent study throughout the week. The best use of this devotional is as a way to stimulate you to go to God's Word, as it is His Word that changes hearts.

May I suggest how to use this devotional? Read the devotion early in the week, and then study the accompanying passages. You will find that the amount of reading varies each week. What's important is not the amount you read but that you reflect and pray about what you have read. In each week's devotion, you will always find suggested reading to be the section of Scripture surrounding that week's key passage. This is so the passage will be understood in its appropriate context, an extremely important issue related to the study and application of God's Word. The other suggested Scripture readings vary but relate also to the key passage or theme of the devotion for that particular week. Refer back to the devotion as often as you desire. Throughout the week, ask yourself a few questions as it relates to your study: first, what biblical truth is God impressing upon my heart? Second, what am I learning about the character of God? Third, how might God desire to change me?

Spiritual growth occurs day by day as we encounter God. If you already have a pattern of daily Scripture reading, let *Unveiled* be a supplement. If you don't, let this devotional be an inspiration to begin one. Through it all, my hope and prayer is that as you proceed through *Unveiled*, the Holy Spirit will be at work in your life, giving you the desire to "taste" more and more of God. After all, what better nourishment than the spiritual nourishment that comes from God's Word? "Oh, taste and see that the LORD is good" (Psalm 34:8).

Week 1

Unveiled

And we all, with unveiled face, beholding the glory of the Lord, are being transformed into the same image from one degree of glory to another. For this comes from the Lord who is Spirit.
—2 Corinthians 3:18

Moses entered the presence of God without wearing a veil, but when he returned to the people of Israel, he veiled himself. One reason Moses wore a veil in the presence of the Israelites was because God's glory shined so brightly from his face that it frightened them. Paul explains in 2 Corinthians that the veil was also worn to indicate the fading glory of the old covenant, the Mosaic system. Under the old covenant, repeated sacrifices had to be made to atone for the people's sins. Paul knew the old covenant was ineffective in changing people's hearts and instead emphasized that freedom to obey the law came from the power of the Holy Spirit. "Now the Lord is Spirit, and where the Spirit of the Lord is, there is freedom" (2 Corinthians 3:17).

"And we all, with unveiled face, beholding the glory of the Lord, are being transformed into the same image from one degree of glory to another. For this comes from the Lord who is Spirit" (2 Corinthians 3:18). The Greek word translated as the English *beholding* can mean "behold," "reflect," or to "look at in the mirror," but its use in the above passage has to do with removing that which impedes one's ability to see God's glory. In this passage, it was removing the veil. For the Jewish people, the law was what impeded them from seeing God's glory, as their hearts remained "veiled" because they rejected Jesus Christ as the Messiah. As Paul saw it, the new covenant far exceeded the glory of the old because it is what could truly bring people into a right standing before God, or righteousness. So in essence, Paul was saying what the old covenant (Mosaic system) could not accomplish, Jesus Christ could and did.

Second Corinthians 3:18 serves as the title verse for *Unveiled* because as Christians we should not just have as our desire to be saved *from* something, that something being hell, but *to* something, an abundant life in Christ Jesus. Though never perfect until we go to be with the Lord, as we behold the Lord through the ministry of the Holy Spirit in our lives, we grow into more mature Christians. This is commonly referred to as the doctrine of sanctification. Sanctification means to "set apart," and in one sense, when we come to faith in Christ, we are set apart. There is, however, another part of the sanctification process that takes place over time whereby Christians grow in their Christ likeness.

In his commentary on 2 Corinthians, author Kent Hughes says "We express the image of God by living according to the commandments, which express His nature. The change is progressive, so that willing exposure to the sunlight of God's presence will burn His image ever deeper into our character and will."

As you and I, with love for God being our motive, undertake the effort to know Him more by spending time in His Word and by obedience to His will, the Holy Spirit will work to make us more like Christ. Is that what you desire? I hope it is. Is that what God expects? Yes. Is that what He deserves? Absolutely! When our lives are changed by the gospel and we reflect more and more each day the image of Christ, guess who gets the glory? God gets it, just as it should be.

I hope this devotional, but more importantly the accompanying Scriptures, by the power of the Holy Spirit, transforms you into the person God created you to be. Remember, it is because of Jesus Christ that we are "unveiled."

Prayer

Lord, I pray that by Your power I will be transformed into the person You call me to be. It is a process that on this side of heaven will never end. Let my motives be out of love for You. You gave Your Son, the perfect reflection of You, for my sins. Thank You for removing my veil to behold Your glory. Have Your will in my life each day.

Monday: Exodus 26:31-37, 34:29-35

Tuesday: Hebrews 9:11-10:25; Matthew 27:45-54

Wednesday: Romans 8:29; 2 Corinthians 3:1-18, 4:1-6

Thursday: Romans 12:1-2; Ephesians 4:17-24; Colossians 3:1-11

Friday: Philippians 3:8-14; 1 Thessalonians 5:23-24; Hebrews 13:20-21

Week 2

Does Your Past Predict Your Future?

For you have heard of my former life ... how I persecuted the church of God violently and tried to destroy it.
—Galatians 1:13

My dad is a former educator who retired as a principal some years ago. Still today, he likes to keep up with what goes on in the education system where he served and where I grew up. In doing so, he has met some of the current school principals in our hometown. On one occasion he met a woman who serves as principal at one of the local high schools. In speaking with her over time, they came to realize that she was someone with whom I attended high school. At one point, she told my dad that many of her high school friends never would have believed she would end up being a principal, and though I didn't know her well, I wouldn't have imagined it either. I guess in all of our pasts, there are things that may seem as if they should disqualify us from some future position or perhaps service. But is that really how it should be?

"For you have heard of my former life…how I persecuted the church of God violently and tried to destroy it" (Galatians 1:13). Paul was on the "fast track" in Judaism, extremely zealous over his religion, advancing rapidly and outpacing others his age (Galatians 1:14). He was also the premier persecutor of the church, a killer of Christians. He approved the execution of Stephen, the first Christian martyr (Acts 8:1). Who could have imagined that Paul would become what he became to the church of Jesus Christ? I believe after Paul's conversion, though he understood well the graciousness of God, it still amazed him greatly that He would use him in the way he did. In writing to the church at Corinth, Paul even admitted that he was indeed unworthy to be an apostle because of all he had done against the church (1 Corinthians 15:9). God, however, in His providence, had other plans from the very beginning. He knew exactly what Paul would become to the church. Paul gives testimony to that, proclaiming God had set him apart before he was born, called him by His grace, and revealed Jesus to him (Galatians 1:15-16). So the biggest persecutor of the church of Jesus Christ became the biggest builder of the church of Jesus Christ. How amazing!

It's sometimes easy for you and me to look at a person's past and to think there are certain things he or she will never do or be. That was the case with my schoolmate who became a principal. And I am sure that was the case with the apostle Paul. Fully aware of Paul's reputation as a persecutor of Christians, Ananias was even hesitant to obey the Lord and go to Paul after Paul's conversion (Acts 9:13). Is it not striking that Paul's conversion is recorded three times in the book of Acts? Why might that be? Could it be possible that the Holy Spirit, through the inspired pen of Luke, wants us to know of the abundant grace of our Savior? Is it perhaps to demonstrate through the example of Paul that no one is beyond God's saving hand? It may very well be. So, is a person's past a predictor of their future service to God?

The story of the apostle Paul would indicate the answer is no. God's grace is unimaginable, and the apostle Paul is a great example of that grace, but you and I are as well. We needed God's grace in salvation, and we continue to need His grace each day of our lives. Don't presume to know who may be beyond the grace of God. And never deny showing others the grace God has shown you. Let the past lie in the past because once changed by Jesus Christ, whether it's the apostle Paul, you, me, or anyone else, the future is eternal.

Prayer

God, You are gracious. Paul received it and then proclaimed it, but it all comes from what Your Son, Jesus Christ, did on the cross. You showed me that same grace. Lord, my prayer is that I will truly appreciate and accept it. Give me the desire to show that grace to others each day. Keep me close to you this day, Lord, and help me do Your will.

Monday: Galatians 1:1-24
Tuesday: Acts 7:1-8:3
Wednesday: Acts 9:1-31
Thursday: Acts 21:37-22:16, 26:12-18
Friday: 1 Corinthians 15:1-11; 1 Timothy 1:12-17

Week 3

Does Our View of God Define Him?

For my thoughts are not your thoughts, neither are your ways my ways, declares the LORD. For as the heavens are higher than the earth, so are my ways higher than your ways and my thoughts than your thoughts.
—Isaiah 55:8-9

Some years ago I read a commentary on Psalm 8 where the writer told a story about a new building that was to be constructed at Harvard University. Among the things included in the original design of this building was an inscription at the entrance that read, "Man is the measure of all things." It seems that still to this day, man believes he is the measure of all things. Why do I say that? As I bought a cup of coffee on October 7, 2010, I noticed the headline of *USA Today*, which read "How America Sees God." My first thought before even reading the article was, *I wonder how God sees America.* This article was based on a book by two Baylor University sociologists, who, through telephone interviews, collected people's views of God and categorized them according to four different views. The four views of God were (1) an authoritative God who judges human behavior, sometimes punishing unfaithfulness; (2) a benevolent God who sees His handiwork but is less likely to judge and punish human behavior; (3) a critical God who is judgmental but rarely acts on earth, instead reserving final judgment for the afterlife; and (4) a distant God who set everything in motion and then let it go, not having clear concerns about activities or world events. The survey results showed each of the four views of God pretty evenly represented by Americans. The article also noted that our view of God often shapes our attitude on keys issues in the world today.

"For my thoughts are not your thoughts, neither are your ways my ways, declares the LORD" (Isaiah 55:8). My intention is not to spend a great deal of time analyzing the contents of the article but to instead challenge the whole premise of our ability, outside of the study of God's Word, to attempt to define Him. Who are we to think we can measure God outside of who He tells us He is? In Isaiah 55, the prophet Isaiah says we are invited to enter into the blessings that God has promised. The immediate context of Isaiah 55:8-9 was the need for man to exchange his wicked ways and unrighteous thoughts for God's: "For as the heavens are higher than the earth, so are my ways higher than your ways and my thoughts than your thoughts."

Humans are finite creatures, unable to describe God or fully comprehend Him. We know Him in the sense of a relationship through salvation, but our knowledge is limited and imperfect. As to the story I referenced earlier concerning the proposed inscription "Man is the measure of all things," well, it never happened because the president of Harvard had other ideas, having it replaced with "What is man that you are mindful of him?" (Psalm 8:4). What a gracious God we have, considering that being so much higher and greater than you or I, He is still mindful of us.

Why is it that we search all over to find out who God is when His Word reveals that for us? We don't need a survey or anything else, only His Spirit-inspired Word. Our view of God does determine our response to Him, but in no way is it His measure. This article also had no mention of Jesus Christ, the incarnate God. Our knowledge of God in salvation comes only by knowing Jesus Christ. Listen to Jesus' own words: "All things have been handed over to me by my Father, and no one knows the Son except the Father, and no one knows the Father except the Son and anyone to whom the Son chooses to reveal him" (Matthew 11:27). True knowledge of God comes by way of the Son, revealed to us by the Holy Spirit. All revealed in His Word and not at all dependent on mine, yours, or anyone else's perceptions.

Prayer

Father, there have been many times when I have tried to define You outside of how You disclose Yourself in Your Word. Forgive me! I'm thankful that Your ways are higher than my ways and Your thoughts are higher than my thoughts because my ways and my thoughts are sinful. Help me submit to how You have defined Yourself in the Scriptures. Thank You that I can know You through Your Son, Jesus Christ. Keep me humble before You each and every day.

Monday: Isaiah 55:1-13
Tuesday: Isaiah 40:1-31
Wednesday: Psalm 8:1-9
Thursday: Psalm 113:1-9, 145:1-21
Friday: Ephesians 3:20-21; Romans 11:33-36

Week 4

But of God

[W]ho were born, not of blood nor of the will of flesh nor of
the will of man, but of God.
—John 1:13

Why do we believe what we do about salvation? Is it tradition? Is it because it makes us feel better about ourselves? Or is it because it makes us feel better about God? Scripture teaches that before we became children of God, we were dead in our trespasses and sins (Ephesians 2:1). Our understanding the context in which a verse of Scripture is contained can never be overemphasized. When the appropriate context is not fully appreciated, one can make the Bible say almost anything. Sure, we believed and we made a decision to accept Jesus Christ as Savior and Lord. No one denies that. The Bible teaches that. The Bible also teaches that humans are responsible for that choice. The question at hand, however, is who it is that initiates our salvation?

Jesus teaches in John 6:44 that no one can come to Him unless the Father draws him or her. Theologically, this is known as an "effectual call," defined as "an act of God the Father, speaking through the proclamation of the gospel, in which He summons people to Himself in such a way that they respond in saving faith." Do you struggle with the fact that you are not the one who initiated your salvation, or do you believe you did? Why is it that as humans, we desire to be the ultimate arbiter of salvation? Why do some staunchly defend man's free will in salvation? Has our religious tradition taught us that? These are all important questions to consider.

"[W]ho were born, not of blood nor of the will of the flesh nor of the will of man, but of God" (John 1:13). In context, this verse tells us that our becoming children of God doesn't depend on our race, gender, or degree of effort on our part but results solely on the sovereign work of God. It is an act of God alone in which He renews the human heart. Give God all the credit for your salvation because what Jesus did in His life, death, and resurrection, He deserves it all.

Aside from God getting all the glory He is due, the best part of our salvation being all of God is that we can't lose it. That's a good thing because if left to ourselves, we would. We were chosen by the Father, who then gave us to the Son. The Son in return promised He would lose nothing the Father had given Him (John 6:39). So how does this promise play out in our lives? It plays out as comfort and security, knowing that God, who is sovereign in salvation, set His heart on you in spite of your being dead in your sins. By sending His Son to purchase you with His blood, He made you His child. And once you are a child of God, you are forever a child of God.

How can we take credit for our salvation knowing this? How the Bible teaches that we are held responsible for our belief or unbelief, and how salvation is all of God will always be beyond our full comprehension, but that is why He is God. In his book *Evangelism and the Sovereignty of God*, J. I. Packer says "our speculations are not the measure of our God."

Let us apply the promised truth of this verse. Let God be God, let Scripture contain mystery, and let us realize that our understanding it is not the measure of its truth. After all, He alone is God!

Prayer

Father God, thank You for setting Your love on me and bringing me to salvation. I am so grateful that my salvation is all of You because if it resulted from my effort, I would lose it. Help me accept by faith things I can't fully comprehend but always know I can trust Your Word. Amen.

Monday: John 1:1-18
Tuesday: John 3:1-21
Wednesday: Romans 9:1-29
Thursday: Ephesians 2:1-10; Titus 3:1-7
Friday: 1 John 2:28-3:3; 1 Peter 1:3-12

Week 5

No Other Way

I am the way, and the truth, and the life. No one comes to the Father except through me.
—John 14:6

Not through Buddha, Mohammad, Mormonism, the Mosaic Law, or good works. There is only one way to spend eternity in heaven, and that is through faith in Jesus Christ. There is a difference between tolerance and having a firm conviction about something. People are not intolerant because they stand firm on the exclusivity of Jesus Christ as the only way to the Father. Just because our culture and our media say so doesn't make it true. The truth is that the claims of Christ are exclusive, and as Christians, we cannot waver on this issue. I know some people who, when I look at their character and kindness, even knowing they are of a religion other than Christianity, I think, *How can those people not be saved, or why wouldn't God save them?* God can save them, but that salvation will not come based on their goodness but only by grace through faith in Jesus Christ.

We are not left to guess who Jesus claimed to be. One of the primary purposes for which John wrote his gospel was so people would believe Jesus is the Messiah, the Christ. For the Jews, the "Messiah" represented the coming "anointed one" who would save God's people. The book of John records seven "I am" statements that Jesus made in which He explicitly claimed to be God. These "I am" statements angered the religious leaders of Jesus' day because they understood that this was the covenant name of God first disclosed to Moses (Exodus 3:14). While all of the "I am" statements were and are controversial, perhaps none is more despised than the one we find in John 14:6 "I am the way, and the truth, and the life. No one comes to the Father except through me." Jesus' claim of deity and exclusivity bring about an angry reaction today. I can hear it now, "Jesus can't be the only way; I believe there are many ways." But Jesus didn't say that. He's not just one of the ways but "the way." Does that offend you? I hope not, but make no mistake, it offends many.

Unfortunately, even many Christians are subtly being broken down as to their conviction on the exclusive claims of Jesus Christ. It just doesn't fit our culture in this era of tolerance that such exclusivity could be claimed. But

Jesus was never interested in fitting into the norm of society. His claims were always bold, to the point, and unapologetic. It may seem that not believing in and expressing the exclusive claims of Christ with confidence appear more humble and gracious, attributes that do please our Lord, but Jesus desires we take Him at His word. If we waver on this issue, and in effect deny its truth, it's His heart we break. The truths of Jesus' words are never dependant on how they make us feel.

So how must a Christian proceed? Take Jesus' words at face value. He said it and He meant it, so don't crumble in the name of tolerance. Trust in the authority of Jesus' words. Do you think He died for you not to believe Him?

Prayer

Dear Lord, thank You that You are the way, the only way to be reconciled to the Father. Help me to lovingly but boldly stand firm on what Your Word says, that through no other way but faith in Your work can one be made right with God. As society more and more counters Your claims, God, give me strength to proclaim the truth.

Monday: John 14:1-14; Exodus 3:13-15
Tuesday: John 6:22-40, 8:12-20
Wednesday: John 10:1-18, 11:17-27
Thursday: John 15:1-17
Friday: John 8:48-58; Acts 4:10-12

Week 6

Where Theology and Experience Meet

For our sake he made him to be sin who knew no sin, so that in him we might become the righteousness of God.
—2 Corinthians 5:21

Many Christians have sung 2 Corinthians 5:21 from the popular contemporary Christian song "Jesus Messiah" by Chris Tomlin. It is a great worship song that contains sound theology, but I have two questions as it relates to 2 Corinthians 5:21. First, do you understand the truth being taught in this verse? Second, have you embraced that truth?

This is a verse in which I believe theology and experience meet. Let me explain. Some say we shouldn't worry so much about theology because it takes away from a true "experience" with God in worship. On the other hand, in an attempt to guard theology so tightly, others resist any sort of "experience" with God in worship, believing it somehow undermines an appreciation of theology. However, when we appropriately apply this verse, it should lead to both. Scripture teaches that "while we were still sinners, Christ died for us" (Romans 5:8). In this section of 2 Corinthians, Paul describes the greatness of God's love and the answer as to how we are reconciled to Him. That answer culminates with the most beautiful truth of verse 21: "For our sake He made Him to be sin who knew no sin, so that in Him we might become the righteousness of God" (2 Corinthians 5:21).

It truly was for our sake, because God didn't need us for anything, but He loved us so much that He made "Him"—Jesus—"sin." Jesus was sinless, and by becoming sin for us, we became "the righteousness of God." Righteousness means to be in a right standing with God; it is what is right and just. Known as the doctrine of justification, it is a legal term whereby one is declared not guilty before God.

I once heard 2 Corinthians 5:21 explained this way: "Though Jesus wasn't a sinner, on the cross, God treated Him as if He was. On the other hand, though we're not righteous, God treats us as if we are. So, in essence, on the cross, God treated Jesus as if He had lived our life so He could treat us as if we had lived His." This verse also supports the doctrine of atonement, which is the work Jesus did in His life and death to earn our salvation. Christ was our substitute and took on our sin that we might be given His righteousness.

So you ask, "What do you mean by theology and experience meeting?" The point is simply this: we can have an experience and have it not be based on right theology. An "experience" void of right theology never leads to proper worship or God's glory. However, when you grasp and fully embrace the theological truth of 2 Corinthians 5:21, realizing that because of the atoning sacrifice of Christ, your position before God is perfect, you will "experience" God and your worship will change. You will no longer be paralyzed by your past, present, or future failures because this verse tells you that they are completely paid for. What freedom when you realize God loves you this much! And because He loves you, you love Him, and your motivation to serve and worship Him will be pleasing to Him because it comes not out of duty but gratitude. Theology, meet experience.

Prayer

Father, I can't believe You love me that much, but You do. Thank You. I know my sin put Jesus on the cross, but He bore it willingly. As I live today, with my failures before me, help me grasp that my position before You, God, is perfect, because my Savior is perfect. Never let me move beyond the cross. Let it motivate me to live for Your glory each day, thankful Jesus chose to be my substitute.

Monday: 2 Corinthians 5:1-21
Tuesday: Isaiah 53:1-12
Wednesday: Romans 3:21-31, 5:12-21
Thursday: Galatians 3:10-14; Hebrews 4:14-16; 1 Peter 2:13-25
Friday: 1 John 2:1-6

Week 7

Perfect Peace

You keep him in perfect peace whose mind is stayed on you.
—Isaiah 26:3

Total trust and reliance on someone can be an elusive thing. If it comes at all, it only comes as a result of knowing someone intimately, but even then, it is wavering at best. Perhaps in your past someone important to you let you down, hardening you to the idea of having that one person whose words can put you at peace. Well, as hard as you may look, you will never find that person.

Isaiah 26:1-15 is a song of praise to God for delivering a redeemed remnant (a part of a larger whole) of Judah. "You keep him in perfect peace whose mind is stayed on you" (Isaiah 26:3). In context, the "perfect peace" Isaiah writes of is in reference to peace for the city of Jerusalem and the nation of Israel. One of the major themes of the book of Isaiah is to trust in the LORD, and Isaiah challenges Israel to do that very thing, "Trust in the LORD forever" (Isaiah 26:4).

This "perfect peace," however, also refers to peace as individuals. For the most part, in some form or fashion, people long for peace. Unfortunately, we often look for it in all the wrong places. Too often we look for it in things we can see, feel and touch. So, what is true peace? First, true peace, peace with God, comes only through salvation. Before we were reconciled to God by the death of Christ, "we were enemies" (Romans 5:10). To be "stayed" on, also translated as "steadfast" means to "lean on" or "rely upon". In this passage, Isaiah is talking about a "peace" that is a result of a person's mind leaning and relying on God. The Hebrew word for "mind" has to do with inclination, disposition, and motivation. It is what one is inclined toward and motivated by and is, thereby, his or her natural disposition.

Is your mind "stayed" on the LORD? Are you steadfast in seeking the peace that He alone provides, or are you seeking peace apart from Him? Maybe peace the world offers. You know; the peace that never remains and is always conditional. Who are you going to lean on today? Maybe it is your family or your friends, and sure, they can and should be of great comfort to you. But today and every day make the LORD your priority. Be steadfast and keep your mind stayed on the LORD because His peace is a peace "which surpasses all understanding" (Philippians 4:7). Today, lean on the LORD and He will give you "perfect peace" because He Himself is perfect.

Prayer

Dear Lord, I pray for Your "perfect peace." I pray that my heart's desire will be to keep my mind "stayed" on You. I know it is the only way I can have the peace of God that surpasses all understanding. Thank You for my Savior, Jesus Christ. It is "in Him" where peace is found. Amen!

Monday: Isaiah 26:1-21
Tuesday: Isaiah 9:6, 11:6-9, 53:1-6
Wednesday: John 14:15-31, 16:25-33
Thursday: Romans 5:1-11; Ephesians 2:11-22
Friday: Philippians 4:4-9

Week 8

Guarding the Good Deposit

Guard the good deposit entrusted to you.
—2 Timothy 1:14

If you knew you were going to die, what would you want to say to those you love the most? What would you most want them to know? There is no doubt that Paul loved Timothy. Aside for his love for the Lord, you would be hard-pressed to find anyone Paul loved more. They had spent years together as ministers of the gospel. At the time of Paul's writing, Timothy was in Ephesus in order to deal with a difficult situation within the church. Paul was imprisoned in Rome for the second and last time. So, at the end of his life, Paul chose to write Timothy to encourage and exhort him to stand firm and be faithful as he carried on in ministry.

Much of the first chapter of Paul's letter is spent encouraging Timothy to use the gift God had given him and not to be ashamed of the gospel, "the testimony about our Lord" (2 Timothy 1:8). Timothy's struggles in Ephesus were discouraging him, and he appeared weary. Paul reminded Timothy how he had suffered for the sake of the gospel during his ministry. Timothy had witnessed much of that suffering. In verses 8-10, Paul even provided a summary of the gospel itself. Paul knew in his heart that Timothy understood the theological parameters of the gospel, but he still exhorted him to follow the example he had set and to guard the gospel of Jesus Christ.

"Guard the good deposit entrusted to you" (2 Timothy 1:14). The "good deposit" is the truth of the gospel. In this last letter, Paul was leaving Timothy with the responsibility to see that the gospel not become "lost" or "watered down." He warned him about listening to opposing views and godless chatter from false teachers. 2 Timothy has been referred to as Paul's "last will and testament" to the church. This is because it carries an important message to the contemporary church today, not only to pastors, but to each of us who minister. All Christians are called to minister. As to what kind of minister you are, however, is up to you. We live in a world today where God's Word is being marginalized in so many aspects of our culture. Many say that it has never been harder to be a Christian than it is today, but considering Paul's letter to Timothy, that's not necessarily the case. There has always been resistance to the gospel of Jesus Christ. There always will be.

Though resistance to the gospel may be an ever-present reality, be encouraged by Paul's message. Note the beginning of verse 14: "By the Holy Spirit who dwells in us." Your ministry is never by your power but by the power of Holy Spirit working through you. Paul knew human strength would not be enough for Timothy to accomplish what God had called him to. In fact, Timothy was rather timid by nature and was young relative to many within the church. So as Timothy's opposition in Ephesus came from prominent members in the church, it was only God's power that he could rely on.

It is the same with us. By the power of the Holy Spirit, "guard the good deposit" and rely on His strength, even when others oppose you and the difficulty is great. As people try to distort the gospel, guard it! As they try to minimize it, elevate it. Right doctrine matters because it leads to right doing. Have a high regard for the Gospel.

Prayer

Lord, thank You for the Gospel. Give me strength today to
not shrink back from the truth of Your Word. No matter how unreceptive
our world is to Your truth, help me to be faithful to guard it—not just part
of it but the whole of it. Help me to never compromise it in my own life.
Thank You for grace in doing so. Thank You for all the faithful men and
women who proclaim it and live it each day. Most of all, thank You for
Christ.

Monday: 2 Timothy 1:1-14
Tuesday: 2 Timothy 2:1-13
Wednesday: 1 Timothy 6:11-21
Thursday: 1 Corinthians 9:1-23
Friday: Galatians 1:11-2:10

Week 9

God Knows

For I have many in this city who are my people.
—Acts 18:10

It must have been heartbreaking for Paul that the message of the gospel he proclaimed upon his conversion was rejected by so many of his fellow Jews. Paul began his second missionary journey by revisiting some of the churches he founded in Galatia during his first journey. He then went to Macedonia and Achaia, now present-day Greece. It was during this part of Paul's travels that he came to the city of Corinth, a large, influential, but very corrupt and immoral city. As was his custom, Paul could be found reasoning with the Jews in the synagogue, testifying that Jesus was the Christ. Opposition to Paul was constant, and in most cases, the opposition was so hostile that he was forced to leave the general area in which he was preaching. Opposition occurred on this occasion as well, with Paul finally indicating that the people themselves were responsible for their sins, saying to them, "Your blood be on your own heads!" He then proclaimed that from then on he would go to the Gentiles. This time, however, Paul did not leave town but went to the house next to the synagogue.

Paul knew it was God who did the saving, and as he witnessed on this occasion, some came to saving faith, but others of course did not. But Paul was also human, and such a constant presence of opposition and danger had to be discouraging at times. Appearing in need of encouragement, encouragement is what Paul got, and it came in a vision from the Lord. The Lord told Paul not to be afraid but to continue to speak and not be silent, reassuring him, "I am with you, and no one will attack you to harm you" (Acts 18:10a).

Assurance of the Lord's presence and protection while in Corinth was certainly encouraging to Paul and should encourage you and me as well. Paul remained in Corinth for a year and a half. But there is something else that is of great encouragement in this verse: "for I have many in this city who are my people" (Acts 18:10b). God knows His own. He knew there were those in Corinth Paul had yet to encounter with the gospel of Jesus Christ that would come to saving faith. And God knows those today who are His, those who through the hearing of the gospel will be brought to saving faith.

Faith is a gift from God, but human effort as we live out that faith is not incompatible with it. God uses humans as means to fulfill His purposes. In this passage, God wasn't looking backward; He was looking forward. Paul's responsibility was to proclaim the gospel; the saving was left to God. Salvation is not a secret to God because He predestined it to be, and predestined that it would only be by faith in Jesus Christ.

Note Paul's response to God's vision. It didn't make him passive about what he was to do in the city of Corinth, or anywhere else in which he ministered. God's sovereignty in salvation doesn't limit our role or responsibility to proclaim the gospel. There remains a "holy seed" in need of its hearing. We don't know who God will choose to save and we're not the ones responsible for the saving. Our calling is plain and simple: proclaim the message of Christ and trust the Lord for the rest. Thank God He has taken that pressure off us. Let our prayer be that this will free you and me to proclaim His message with more fervency than ever before.

Prayer

Dear Father, thank You that You have made a way of salvation through Your Son, Jesus Christ. Thank You that You allow me to participate in Your plan of salvation. Father, thank You most of all that You have chosen a people for Yourself in spite of our sin. Help us fulfill our role and to diligently proclaim Your message to those You have predestined to save.

Monday: Acts 18:1-17
Tuesday: 2 Timothy 2:1-13
Wednesday: Ephesians 1:3-14
Thursday: John 10:14-16
Friday: Romans 10:14-17

Week 10

Blessed through Suffering

The LORD gave, and the LORD has taken away;
blessed be the name of the LORD.
—Job 1:21

First Job's property was taken, and then his children were killed, and if that was not enough, Satan attacked his health. How in the world could Job utter the words recorded in 1:21 of the book that bears his name after all that happened? Here's the questions we are to consider: Is God's goodness dependent only on how well our life goes, or is He still good when He strips certain things away, causing us to suffer?

I go to church with a man named Jack Lavallet. I can't say I know Jack overly well, but we did have an opportunity to spend some time together while taking classes toward our master's degrees. Jack had several noticeable characteristics: he always smiled, was always gracious, and there was no doubt in my mind he loved the Lord. Nothing has changed. These were and still are constants with Jack.

But there is another constant in Jack's life. He is paralyzed. Jack was paralyzed as a result of an accident in college when he dived into the shallow end of a swimming pool. A few years ago I had the opportunity to hear Jack share his testimony before our church. I was really struck when he said, "The LORD loved me enough to crush me." As Jack described this event in his life, he indicated that in one single moment, having just gone off to college, he went from a newfound independence to total dependence.

"…The LORD gave, and the LORD has taken away; blessed be the name of the LORD" (Job 1:21) But Job was a righteous man, "blameless and upright, one who feared God and turned away from evil" (Job 1:1). Now, there are some differences between God allowing Job to suffer and His allowing Jack to. In fact, Jack would probably cringe at the comparison to Job because in contrast to Job's righteousness, at the time of Jack's injury, he was not living a life very pleasing to God. What they do have in common is the ultimate purpose for each of their suffering, God's glory. You might ask, "How can God be glorified in that?" The answer is that God used Job's suffering to display Himself more fully to Job, while He used Jack's suffering to draw Jack to Him. In both cases, God's glory resulted.

Though we often like to avoid those passages that tell of suffering, the Bible clearly teaches that both the righteous and the unrighteous suffer. Scripture also teaches that God is sovereign over all of it. When suffering strikes, it can be a hard truth to accept, but it's still the truth. God has Satan on a string, and Satan could only do to Job what God allowed him to do. Now, unlike Job, the LORD didn't take Jack's property or his children. The LORD took away Jack's ability to walk and everything that goes along with it. Everything you and I take for granted. There were for Job, and I am sure for Jack as well, times of doubt and questioning.

At the end of the book of Job, we find that the LORD restored Job's fortunes (Job 42:10). He has yet to restore Jack's paralysis, but one day, He will (Romans 8:23). Jack's injury was Jack's rescue.

So, does God's goodness depend on whether or not He allows us to suffer? Or does the blessing come most completely after the point of breaking? I believe Jack would testify to the latter. Understanding God's purpose in everything is not easy; in fact, it is impossible. But accepting that He is sovereign and good is clearly taught in His Word. Never doubt God's purposes for allowing your pain. Believe God will give you grace through it, believe it ultimately works for your good, but most of all, believe that it works for God's glory.

Prayer

Dear God, thank You for all the faithful people who have glorified You as they suffered. They testify to Your goodness and grace. Your Word tells us that suffering comes. It is never easy, but by the power of the Holy Spirit, I can endure it graciously. Help me to do that. I know You are not only in control of suffering, but You are with me as I go through it. Help me realize that each and every day, no matter my circumstance, You are all I need.

Monday: Job 1:1-2:10
Tuesday: Job 38:1-40:24
Wednesday: Job 41:1-42:17; Psalm 34:19
Thursday: Acts 14:19-23; Romans 5:3-5; 2 Corinthians 4:7-18
Friday: 1 Thessalonians 2:17-3:5; James 1:2-12; 1 Peter 4:12-5:11

Week 11

The Greater Vision of the LORD

For the LORD sees not as man sees: man looks on the outward
appearance, but the LORD looks on the heart.
—1 Samuel 16:7

God, why did You make me like you did? Why didn't You give me that gift or that talent? Whether young or old, this is perhaps a question you have posed to the LORD, or at least wondered yourself. When I was in elementary school there was a guy named Joey who played on the high school football team. I wanted to be him so much that for a time, I signed my first name using his rather than my own.

How many of us look around and wish we were in another person's position, maybe as it relates to physical appearance, skill, or perhaps circumstance? "I wish I had what that person has: more money, a more prominent career, or perhaps a vacation home. Or maybe if I was just more athletic, maybe that superstar on the football team, that would make life perfect." In no way are any of these gifts things to be ashamed of. Just give God the glory for it and honor Him as you use them.

As humans, we all have an innate desire to be accepted, and unfortunately, from the world's perspective, the things listed above often bring that acceptance. The question is, should they? Does that really constitute true acceptance?

"For the LORD sees not as man sees: man looks on the outward appearance, but the LORD looks on the heart" (1 Samuel 16:7) Saul's problem was not his physical appearance, for he was handsome and tall, just like one might picture a king. Saul's problem was his heart, and that was the reason God rejected him as king. When he should have been leading the people of Israel to obey God, he himself lacked obedience.

As chapter 16 of 1 Samuel began, the LORD rebuked Samuel for mourning over Saul's rejection as king. Saul was Israel's king because the people demanded one, but David was God's chosen king. What was it the LORD saw in David? Without informing him of which son He had anointed to be king, the LORD instructed Samuel to go to Bethlehem. He told him to find Jesse, "for I have provided for myself a king among his sons" (1 Samuel 16:1).

Jesse had eight sons. What's your guess as to how this story goes? As you might imagine, both Samuel and Jesse saw things differently than the LORD did. The first brother mentioned to replace Saul was Eliab, and immediately Samuel was ready to settle for him saying, "Surely this is the LORD'S anointed" (1 Samuel 16:6). Eliab was the oldest and was like Saul in appearance, a strong physical presence. Some things never change.

In society today, that is exactly how it works. Not to deny that certain skills and attributes aren't important for certain things, but we have this preconceived idea that we know, oftentimes by physical appearance or charisma, the best qualities of a person. In essence, the priorities of particular attributes are often mixed up. Much was the case in this story as Jesse paraded seven of his sons by Samuel. One by one the LORD rejected them all as king, which led Samuel to ask Jesse if these were all of his sons. Jesse then mentioned David, the youngest who was keeping the sheep. When David arrived, the LORD said to Samuel, "Arise, anoint him, for this is he" (1 Samuel 16:12).

We see in this text an important attribute of God, His omniscience: He sees and knows all. While Samuel and Jesse were looking at the outward attributes of these sons, the LORD was looking at the heart, and it was David's heart that was most important to Him. Our heart is what the LORD is looking at when He looks at us as well. Thankfully, God's standard is different from the worlds. His are based on what comes from inside us, not outside. So just as with David, it is our heart that takes priority with God.

So how do we deal in our own lives, or answer that person who believes the world is the measure of his or her self worth? It's often a difficult task. But know this: if you don't answer it, the world will, and more often than not with the wrong answer. We answer it in the same way we answer any question: by going to the only trustworthy source we have, God's Word.

As to the question at hand, we can use this story of David's anointing, the fact that the LORD did not see as Samuel and Jesse did. The LORD knew that faithfulness to Him could not be predicted by what could be seen outwardly. David wasn't perfect, but he was a man after God's own heart. So as we address this issue about our innate desire to be accepted—well, are you a person after God's own heart? If you are, there's good news! You are accepted.

Prayer

God, thank You that You don't see as the world sees. Help me see as You do and to reassure others that it is their heart that truly matters. Amen!

Monday: 1 Samuel 15:1-35
Tuesday: 1 Samuel 16:1-23
Wednesday: Isaiah 55:8-9; 1 Chronicles 28:1-21
Thursday: Psalm 147:10-11; Jeremiah 17:5-10
Friday: Proverbs 4:23; Mark 7:21-23; Luke 6:45; 1 Thessalonians 2:4

Week 12

Well Built?

A pillar and buttress of the truth.
—1 Timothy 3:15

Some of the most difficult challenges for a church do not necessarily come from the secular community but from within the church itself. Such was the case in the church at Ephesus.

After his release from his first imprisonment in Rome, Paul revisited some of the churches in which he had previously ministered, Ephesus among them. Paul determined that it was best to leave Timothy in Ephesus to deal with some of the problems that were coming from within the church leadership. The problem was false teaching, and although the specific content of the false teaching is hard to ascertain, Paul impressed upon Timothy the need to preach the truth and to encourage the members of the church to live out the implications of the gospel. When referring to "a pillar and buttress of the truth" (1 Timothy 3:15), the "truth" Paul was referring to in this verse is the truth of the gospel.

Each Sunday our pastor says, "The church is not the building, it is the people." The people in the church include church leaders such as the pastoral staff, elders, and deacons, but it also includes the lay membership. We are all the church!

Unless you understand architecture, you may not be familiar with the specific purpose a pillar and a buttress serve. Both provide support to a structure, but in slightly different ways. A pillar provides vertical support of a particular structure, whereas a buttress prevents its outward collapse. Buttresses were introduced during the medieval period and were used to support the building of castles. The weight of the stone used to build castles was so heavy that they risked an outward collapse and buttresses helped to prevent that from happening. So the architectural metaphor that Paul uses in this verse as he refers to the "household of God" or the church as a pillar, and buttress is the responsibility that the church has to uphold the truth of the gospel.

The weight of our world today is also heavy. Truth in society has largely become individualized and based on what feels good to the individual. God has given the church the primary responsibility to guard or protect the truth, but unfortunately, many churches have forgotten that responsibility. But we must remember we are the church. The problem with the church at Ephesus was that it was divided against itself. As a member of the body, be careful to do your part not to allow that to happen.

The responsibility to uphold the truth of the gospel of Jesus Christ of course does not fall on the building itself, nor is it solely the responsibility of our pastors, though they certainly lead the way. It is the responsibility of all of us as members of the body of Christ. Truth is not determined by who makes the best case for their opinion being the right or best one. Nor is truth determined by what happens to feel good to the majority of people in our churches. Truth is defined by Scripture. The responsibility Timothy had to the church at Ephesus was to preach the gospel of Jesus Christ and then to exhort the members to live out that gospel. That is also the God-ordained role and responsibility of our pastors today. The Scriptures should define his ministry.

But as the membership, you and I also have a role and responsibility. We are to submit first to God's Word and then to the authority of our church leaders. And then we live it out by teaching and serving others just as Jesus has taught and served you and me. As Christians, we know Jesus Christ is the solid foundation on which the church is built, but let me ask, how solid a structure are you? Pastors, are you well built? Elders and deacons, are you? What about you church member? If today you were to face inspection by the Lord Himself, would He declare you to be "up to code"?

Prayer

Father, I thank You for Your Word. It provides me exactly what I need to be faithful in protecting the truth. I pray the church today will be a pillar and buttress to that truth. Strengthen our pastors today in leading this effort. God, help me serve as a useful member of the body each day, standing firm on Your truth.

Monday: 1 Timothy 3:14-4:5
Tuesday: 1 Timothy 3:1-13
Wednesday: Acts 2:42-47
Thursday: 1 Corinthians 3:1-15
Friday: Luke 6:46-49

Week 13

His Strength

But the Lord stood by me and strengthened me, so that through me
the message might be fully proclaimed.
—2 Timothy 4:17

Paul looked around, and with the exception of Luke, everyone was gone. Evidently, at his "first defense," a type of preliminary hearing, no one stood with Paul. So as the apostle Paul waited to die, he wrote his last words recorded in Scripture to Timothy. It was only natural he would want to express things that would be valuable to Timothy as he carried on in ministry. He wanted to provide some personal instructions, much as he had throughout their years in ministry together. Sure, Paul loved Timothy and wanted him to come soon, but he also wanted Timothy to know something about those he encountered as he ministered. For example, he thought it appropriate for Timothy to be aware of the harm Alexander the coppersmith had done to him, opposing the message of the gospel (2 Timothy 4:14).

As Paul lists these individuals in this section of 2 Timothy, he also wrote about those who were faithful and had left Rome for various reasons. For some of these people there exists little or no historical information to even know where they went or what they did, but that's not the case in verse 9. Here Paul makes clear Demas deserted him and went to Thessalonica, and he wrote that Demas did this because he was "in love with the present world." In essence, for Demas, the heat of Christian ministry had become too much to bear.

This is to be our focus. Scripture doesn't indicate, so there is no need to speculate as to what happened to Demas, but I want us to think about why Demas deserted Paul. Let me repeat what Paul wrote: Demas was "in love with this present world" (2 Timothy 4:10).

How much of that is true today? We make our claims about Christ, do all the things good Christians do, but when we are really called to do something that doesn't fit our perception of what Christianity is, we come to a decision point. When we really get serious, like Paul was, to the calling of God on our lives, it often brings criticism from others. I can hear it now: "That person is over the top; he's taking that religion thing a little too far."

Is that how it happened with Demas? Was the persecution too much for him to take? What about Paul? We know he was willing to "count the cost." Are you willing to count it?

As practically everyone left Paul, he testifies about the One who remained: "But the Lord stood by me and strengthened me, so that through me the message might be fully proclaimed" (2 Timothy 4:17). Paul had always felt God's strength and presence, knowing it was the Lord who propelled him in his calling to proclaim the message of the gospel.

It is the Lord who will strengthen you as well. Believe it! When people desert you, the Lord Jesus will not. He is always faithful. Remember, it's His message, not ours. Go out and fully proclaim the message of Jesus Christ, but do it in His strength, for He is always with you. As Paul had Jesus standing by to rescue him throughout his life, and how this time his rescue would be death, Jesus will stand by and strengthen you as well.

Prayer

Lord, thank You for the strength You gave Paul. Give me that same strength that comes not from me, but like Paul's from You. When the walls close in and criticism comes, help me to not shrink back and be "in love with the present world" but instead to know You are standing by me and that Your strength is the only strength I need. Let me fully proclaim the gospel of Jesus Christ.

Monday: 2 Timothy 4:1-22
Tuesday: 1 Timothy 1:1-20
Wednesday: Acts 18:9-11
Thursday: 2 Corinthians 12:8-10
Friday: Deuteronomy 31:1-8; Joshua 1:1-10; Isaiah 41:8-20

Week 14

Shame

For whoever is ashamed of me and my words ... of him will the
Son of Man also be ashamed.
—Mark 8:38

A few years ago I attended a two-week training session in New Jersey. One of our instructors loved music. Each morning before our sessions began, he would play songs and see if we could guess the artist and title. At some point during our training, he decided to go around the room and have each of us tell the class our favorite type of music and our favorite artist. There were about thirty or so of us in training from around the country, and from the point in the room which he began, my turn came toward the end. I knew the type of music I enjoy. It is contemporary Christian music, and at that time I had been listening a lot to Jeremy Camp. I also recall thinking, as it got closer to my turn to share, *Will I actually say contemporary Christian and Jeremy Camp?*

Well, guess what? I didn't. You see, I was ashamed to be bold about my faith and went the way many do in front of others, a subtle denial perhaps, but still denying my Lord.

Shame can be great and public or it can be subtle, but shame no matter the adjectives is still shame. And God sees it all.

Whose shame is any better known than that of the apostle Peter? The context of this verse is around Jesus' teaching and call to discipleship, and He indicates that those who reject this command will be held accountable at the final judgment. Was there anyone closer to Jesus than Peter? Peter was one of Jesus' disciples. Disciple means "learner," and Peter, as a disciple of Jesus, learned great things from Him. Yet he denied him three times, just as Jesus predicted he would (Mark 14:26-31). Now we know how Peter's story goes, how after he denied Jesus, Peter was restored upon Jesus' resurrection. Peter proved to be a faithful disciple of the Lord as demonstrated at Pentecost and throughout his life. He was faithful to the point of suffering a martyr's death, and as tradition holds, was crucified upside down.

Sometimes our denials of Jesus are subtle. Do people know you are a Christian? Do you proudly claim to be a disciple of Jesus? Or is your faith "private" and just between you and God? It is countercultural for us to do what Jesus clearly calls for us to do: deny, follow, and give up our self-centeredness in allegiance to another. That doesn't fit into the "me, me, me" thinking of our day—or for that matter, Peter's day. Yet it is what Jesus undeniably and unapologetically calls for from you and me.

What is the consequence for not following His call? "For whoever is ashamed of me and my words … of him will the Son of Man also be ashamed" (Mark 8:38). Can you picture Christ's return and the point in which you stand before Him in judgment? What will He say to you? Will it be, "I never knew you, depart from me" (Matthew 7:23)? I pray it won't. Instead, let it be, "Well done, good and faithful servant" (Matthew 25:21). If you have denied Jesus, join the club, because we all have at some point. But like Peter, Jesus graciously stands ready to restore you. Take Jesus' words to us on discipleship seriously, learn from Him each day. Could there be a better teacher?

Prayer

Lord, I know there have been times that I have been ashamed
of You and denied You. What I know even more is that You have witnessed
them all. Forgive me for all of them, Lord, and fill me with Your Spirit, so
I will be bold about my allegiance to You. My desire is to learn from You
each day, so teach me and use me to teach others so the words You say to
me at Your coming will be,
"Well done, good and faithful servant."

Monday: Mark 8:34-9:1
Tuesday: Matthew 16:24-28; Luke 9:23-27
Wednesday: Matthew 7:13-29
Thursday: Matthew 10:24-42
Friday: Luke 12:8-9; 1 John 2:15-27

Week 15

Just Like Judas

So he consented and sought an opportunity to betray him.
—Luke 22:6

I have always loved to hear Royce Collins, a member of our church, read the Scripture passage and pray before our Wednesday night services. I know prayer is not a specific formula of words, but have you ever found there are some people whose prayers just model what prayer should be? Royce's prayers have always seemed to be those types of prayers to me. But tonight, before my pastor preached on Luke 22:1-6 concerning Judas Iscariot's betrayal of Jesus, Royce's prayer was especially striking. At one point, he said, "Lord, the truth is, our feet run fast to do sin." You see, it is really easy to read this passage and look at Judas with complete and utter contempt. "How could he do such a thing? He was so close to Jesus and yet did that? He deserved everything he got."

How often as Christians do we find ourselves looking at the next person, saying, "At least I'm not that bad, I certainly would not sin like he does," when the truth is, our feet often do run fast to sin? Do you believe you are incapable of sin like that of Judas? He betrayed Jesus and plotted with evil men to kill our Lord and Savior. What an awful sin! Our sin may not be as public as Judas's, and it is surely not recorded in Scripture, but our sin put Jesus exactly where Judas plotted with these religious leaders to put him—on the cross. Thankfully, at that cross, Jesus willingly paid that penalty for our sins.

"So he consented and sought an opportunity to betray him …" (Luke 22:6) Think about Judas and the choice he made to seek, at least what he thought was his own gain, and betray Jesus. This plot occurred during Passover, a time when the Israelites commemorated the great mercy God had shown them in sparing the firstborn children of Israel from the death plague incurred by Egypt. Passover occurred once a year as Jews would travel to Jerusalem for a weeklong celebration.

After Judas departed, and Jesus ate the Passover meal with His disciples (the eleven), they left and made their way to the garden of Gethsemane. As He walked with His disciples, Judas came with a crowd and kissed Jesus, normally a custom in which a teacher is greeted by his disciple. But on this occasion, the kiss was an act of betrayal, with the purpose being to identify Jesus. Note Jesus' words to Judas at that moment: "Judas, would you betray the Son of Man with a kiss?" (Luke 22:48). Can you imagine how you might have felt had Jesus spoken those words to you? While attending this prominent Jewish celebration where one of the rituals was the sacrifice of a lamb, Judas, along with the chief priest and scribes were plotting to kill the ultimate Passover Lamb.

Have you betrayed Jesus while faithfully practicing your religious tradition? Have you betrayed your Savior with a kiss? Do your feet run fast to do sin? Don't fall for believing that you are incapable of great sin like Judas. Oh, he seemed so close to the Savior, but in fact, he was very far away. Show Jesus the love that He showed you on the cross. Repent of your betrayal and renew the fellowship that He desires you and I have with Him. After all, He is the Lamb of God and worthy of all honor, glory, and praise.

Prayer

Lord, forgive me when I appear so close to You while my heart is far away. I admit there have been times that I have betrayed You even with a kiss. Let me never be so arrogant to think I am incapable of great sins like Judas. Convict me by Your Holy Spirit when I sin and help me remain close to You each day. Lord, I need Your grace and mercy daily. Thank You for giving it.

Monday: Luke 22:1-23, 22:39-53
Tuesday: Matthew 26:1-25, 26:36-56
Wednesday: Mark 14:1-21, 14:32-50
Thursday: John 13:21-30
Friday: John 18:1-11

Week 16

Through Many Tribulations

Through many tribulations we must enter the kingdom of God.
—Acts 14:22

Every so often in worship we sing the song "Blessed Be Your Name." Note the following lyrics: "Blessed be Your name in the road marked with suffering, though there's pain in the offering blessed be Your name." When reading these lyrics, does it make you ask these questions: "How can I be expected to bless the Lord's name when I am going through times of suffering?" and "How can God be glorified through the suffering of His people?" When hardships arise, these are fairly common questions, and not only among non-Christians but Christians as well.

One of the consequences that results when there is not a biblical understanding as to why suffering occurs is that people begin to question God. They question His control of things and His goodness. The Bible teaches both; He is in control of all things and He is good. At the same time, these questions deserve attention as we minister to others. Fortunately, the Scriptures are not silent in answering them. As we consider this verse, it is important to understand that as Paul and Barnabas traveled on their first missionary journey, they underwent persecution because of their commitment to preaching Christ. "Through many tribulations we must enter the kingdom of God" (Acts 14:22). These words are the testimony of two men who faced significant persecution as they traveled through Galatia. Paul even suffered a stoning in Lystra. It seems a perfect time for Paul to give up his work for the Lord, don't you think? Hardly. As you read of Paul's missionary travels, you will find he often returned through the very areas in which he was persecuted in order to strengthen the churches that had been established.

Contrary to what is often taught, Christians are not immune from the difficulties of this world. Sometimes the difficulties can be worse. Suffering can result from persecution but can also be related to trials that result from a breakdown of relationships, financial woes, or illness, even illnesses that result in death. We must not confuse the issue of tribulation that Luke writes about in this passage with that which is a result of discipline. Though God does allow suffering as discipline for sin, the emphasis of this passage is different. "Though there is pain in the offering, blessed be Your name." What value in our having God's Word to rely upon. Do you find it a comfort? Not only in times of suffering, but at all times, God is sovereignly in control.

In his book *Desiring God*, John Piper uses an analogy of a camera to help explain the idea in which God sees our suffering. He says that on one hand, God uses a narrow lens in which He looks and grieves with us as we undergo suffering. Often, this is the only lens you and I see through. But according to Piper, God also uses another lens, a wide-angle lens in which He sees beyond the immediate situation. This is the lens that sees what has occurred before and what will result from this moment, ultimately working for our good and God's glory. This may happen in our lives as God works out the circumstances, or it may only be realized in death.

So how do we respond during times of tribulation and suffering? We trust in our God, who is sovereign, and we allow His Word to penetrate our shattered and shaken lives. Know that the Bible teaches the reality of suffering, but also know that it teaches that suffering pales in comparison to glory (Romans 8:18). Who better to demonstrate this point than the apostle Paul? Through all of his suffering, Paul knew his strength came from the Lord. As he wrote his final words in 2 Timothy 4:6-8, he was comforted knowing he had fought the good fight, finished the race, and had kept the faith. He also knew what awaited him—a crown of righteousness that the Lord would award him upon His return. That was worth everything Paul had endured in his life on earth.

That crown will be worth everything it cost you in this life as well. Live each day in view of eternity. Be faithful through life's tribulations, knowing we not only have Paul as a model but an even greater one in Jesus Christ, who suffered like no other. We have a great Savior! Worship Him today!

Prayer

Lord, thank You that You can see what I can't. Thank You that the lens of the camera You look through sees beyond what I can imagine. Help me trust that truth each day. Help me trust in Your love and control. Help me get through periods of tribulation and be changed more and more by Your grace into the likeness of Jesus Christ. Amen.

Monday: Acts 13:1-14:28
Tuesday: Psalm 34:19; John 15:18-21
Wednesday: 2 Corinthians 11:21-27; 1 Thessalonians 2:17-3:5
Thursday: 2 Timothy 3:10-12; 1 Peter 4:12-14
Friday: 2 Timothy 4:6-8; Romans 8:18-39

Week 17

Shelter from the Storm

He who dwells in the shelter of the Most High will abide
in the shadow of the Almighty.
—Psalm 91:1

Outside of checking the local forecast, I don't normally watch the *Weather Channel*. The one exception is if I happen to come across an episode of *Storm Stories* while channel surfing. I find some of the episodes fascinating, particularly as they show the intensity of some storms. I guess the weather-related storms, such as hurricanes and tornadoes, fascinate me the most. Hurricanes are those slow-moving storms so deliberate in their approach that unless you have personally experienced one before, you may not believe it could be so powerful. That is, until it arrives with all its fury. On the other hand, tornadoes are often right on top of you before you realize it. Though radar detects their risk, there can be little time to prepare. And what about the devastation they can cause in just a matter of minutes? Images from these episodes on the *Weather Channel* make it clear the destruction these storms cause. Which one presents the greater risk depends on the area of the country in which you live. Part of how people prepare for these storms is by knowing the best places in their homes to take shelter in hopes of remaining safe and secure until the storm passes.

"He who dwells in the shelter of the Most High will abide in the shadow of the Almighty" (Psalm 91:1) Safety and security in the midst of adversity is the central theme of Psalm 91, but it is security that comes from the Lord. The Hebrew word for "dwell" means to be settled. In verse 1, God is referred to as both the "Most High" and "Almighty". When the psalmist refers to God as the "Most High," it emphasizes His strength and sovereignty. We are to be settled in the shelter that only He provides. On the other hand, when God is referred to as "Almighty," the emphasis is on His self-existence, His activity in the world, and His guardianship over our lives. To "abide" means to remain; a faithful person abides or remains in His "shadow," shadow being a metaphor for being under the care and protection of the Almighty.

Storms appear in life as well. Maybe they've appeared in yours. One thing about life storms is that they are indiscriminate. They don't care about geography, social status, income level, race, gender, or anything else. What kind of storm have you encountered? Was it hurricane-like? You know—that slow-moving and progressive storm, maybe a drawn-out illness you or someone you love is battling? Perhaps it was trouble in your marriage that you and your spouse just can't seem to get through. Or was your storm like a tornado—the sudden death or disability of a spouse, child, parent, or friend? Maybe it was the job loss you never saw coming. In all these storms, have you ever considered that just maybe you've been seeking the wrong shelter? God is powerful and sovereign over any storm. He also loves us greatly. When you and I settle in the shelter that He alone provides, He is pleased to keep us in His shadow and see us through any storm. Believe that! If you have been fortunate to thus far be "storm" free, thank God for it, but don't wait until the storm hits to seek His shelter. Seek it now. There is an amazing rest to be found in God. Seek the only shelter that is truly secure.

Prayer

Lord, You are my shelter, the only true security I have. Oftentimes I have sought shelter in things of my making, things I thought would provide protection from any storm. Whatever it may be, if it's not You, it will fail. Lord, You never fail. Praise God!

Monday: Psalm 91:1-16
Tuesday: Psalm 27:1-14
Wednesday: Psalm 31:1-24
Thursday: Psalm 61:1-8, 17:1-15
Friday: Psalm 121:1-8

Week 18

We Can't; He Can

What is impossible with men is possible with God.
—Luke 18:27

Many Christians claim this verse as true yet live as if they don't really believe it at all. Jesus' statement in Luke 18:27 came just after the story of the rich young ruler. Didn't he look just like the kind of person Jesus would want to save? There were some in Jesus' day who believed wealth was a sign of God's favor. Just imagine how much his money could do for advancing the kingdom of God. And by the way, he had also kept the commandments. What a great addition to the kingdom this guy would be. Then Jesus exposed him. When He told him to sell everything and give it to the poor, the rich man couldn't do it. Instead he went away sad. Seeing the man's sadness, Jesus said, "It is easier for a camel to go through the eye of a needle than a rich person to enter the kingdom of God" (Luke 18:25). This prompted some to inquire as to who could be saved. This is the matter we will consider.

"What is impossible with men is possible with God" (Luke 18:27) Salvation is the context in which Jesus made this statement. The issue was not the rich man's wealth, it was his heart. His salvation was not to be based on his works but only on God's grace. You ask, what does this have to do with Christians claiming this verse? What might we take away from Jesus' statement? We are to understand that salvation is in fact only possible with God, and it is possible for anyone. It comes through the person of Jesus Christ. Just as with salvation, every other aspect of Christian ministry is also by God's power. In his book *Absolute Surrender,* John Murray writes, "The whole of Christianity is a work of God's omnipotence."

Let me expand on the point in regard to Christians claiming this verse. We often act as if because it's not possible for us to do something, it's just not possible. When we think this way, much like those who don't believe in God, or those who believe God's power is limited, we are actually denying the whole of who He is. How does that make us any different than those who don't believe or those who have a wrong view of God? It doesn't. We need to live with faith that believes all things are possible with God. Instead of the focus being on the fact that we can't, believe that He can, because He can! Murray goes on to say that too often we learn the first part of this verse, that things are impossible for man, but we never really humble ourselves to learn the second part, that all things are possible with God. He concludes by saying, "Blessed is the man who learns both!" Through belief in an Almighty God, learn the lesson that there is nothing God can't do in and through us, if He so chooses. Trust in that promise this very day because He has given us His Word.

Prayer

Lord, thank You that You assure us that though we are incapable, You are more than capable. The things that are impossible for men are possible with You. Help us believe and trust in these words. We praise You for Your power in salvation and Lord; we ask that Your power continue in our service as witnesses of the gospel of Jesus Christ.

Monday: Luke 18:18-30
Tuesday: Genesis 17:15-16, 18:9-15, 21:1-3
Wednesday: Matthew 19:16-30
Thursday: Mark 10:17-31
Friday: Luke 19:1-10; Ephesians 2:4-10

Week 19

Maturity

Him we proclaim, warning everyone and teaching everyone with all wisdom, that we may present everyone mature in Christ.
—Colossians 1:28

Have you ever heard anyone say, "God wants us to be like a child" and then immediately use a verse like Matthew 18:3 to support their statement, "unless you turn and become like children, you will never enter the kingdom of heaven"? When Jesus spoke these words to His disciples, He was certainly not indicating that there was no need for them to become more spiritually mature. His words were about dependence, humility, trust, and in understanding the need for direction and help. Why is it people take Scripture and use it out of context? There are many reasons, I suppose, but I believe one is that within the church today there are those who cringe when words like *theology* or *doctrine* are emphasized. Theology is the study of God and His relation to the world. Doctrine is defined as what the whole Bible teaches about a particular topic. There seems to be the thought in certain church circles that too great an emphasis on the importance of theology or doctrine only gets in the way of worship. I can hear it now: "Oh, why is all that so important? I just want to worship the Lord." When that's the attitude, I think it's fair to ask who it is they really want to worship.

"Him we proclaim, warning everyone and teaching everyone with all wisdom, that we may present everyone mature in Christ" (Colossians 1:28) A primary emphasis of Paul's ministry was teaching about Christ. It took constant reinforcement on Paul's part in order to keep heresies from infiltrating the church. As Paul wrote from prison in Rome to those in the church at Colossae, it was heretical teaching that he addressed. He had been informed of strange teachings that were threatening the church. Termed the "Colossian heresy," this heresy included elements of pagan mysticism as well as Jewish legalism. It was not that people were trying to do away with Christ in their lives, they simply sought to define Him in a manner of their liking instead of how Jesus revealed Himself and Paul proclaimed Him. A right view of Jesus was critical to faith. It was why Paul labored so hard and suffered so much. It was his central mission; it was why he proclaimed, why he warned, and why he taught. Paul's desire was for those in the church to be "mature" or "perfect" in Christ, knowing this would make it less likely heretical teaching would impact their lives.

That is what the Lord desires for our lives as well. When we deny the value of growing in maturity is when modern day heresies slip into our lives just as they had in Colossae. Those in Colossae had not denied Jesus, they had simply dethroned Him. Paul wanted to assure them that for God to accept them, all they needed was Christ. Christ is all we need as well. Our transformation and maturity, through the power of the Holy Spirit is a process that appreciates the study of theology and doctrine. Worship is not an adversary to the study of theology and doctrine. In fact, worshipping in "spirit and truth" is dependent on proper theology and doctrine. Our right view of Christ is critical. Many people worship in vain because they have a wrong view of Christ. We know Christ in salvation only by His grace, but to grow in maturity of faith requires time and effort. Are you willing to put in that time and effort? Do you see the value? The Lord does want you to be like a child, but it is with an attitude of humility and dependence, knowing we should worship Him according to who He says He is, not who we, in our own pride, sometimes want Him to be. We simply just need to remember, in this life, we're never fully grown!

Prayer

Father, I know my growth comes from the power of the Holy Spirit working in my life. Let me first accept that Your call is a call to a relationship with You and in order to know You,
I must spend time with You. It is through this that You teach me and grow me to a greater and stronger relationship with You. This spiritual maturity helps me live as You call me to live daily, but most of all, it brings You glory. I want to glorify You.

Monday: Colossians 1:1-14
Tuesday: Colossians 1:15-2:5
Wednesday: Ephesians 4:1-16
Thursday: Hebrews 5:11-14
Friday: Philippians 3:1-21

Week 20

My Shepherd

The LORD is my shepherd; I shall not want.
—Psalm 23:1

Many Bible commentary writers acknowledge that Psalm 23 is perhaps the most well-known passage in the Old Testament. It has been referred to as the "most loved song from the inspired pen of David." He wrote it later in his life as he reflected on his days as a shepherd boy. Unlike many of David's psalms, where he expressed wide-ranging emotions, Psalm 23 is full of quiet comfort and confidence in the LORD. One commentary writer says of Psalm 23, "There is no psalm in which the absence of all doubt, misgiving, fear, and anxiety is so remarkable." We would do well in recognizing what David did about our LORD.

"The LORD is my shepherd; I shall not want" (Psalm 23:1). I wonder if we really understand the full impact of what David wrote in this very first verse. The LORD, the Hebrew name "Yahweh," the great "I AM," is my shepherd. This is the name God disclosed to Moses at the burning bush. When Moses asked, "Who are you?" the answer was "I AM WHO I AM" (Exodus 3:14). This is the personal name of God and it refers to His character, the fact that He is eternal and self-existent. He is the God who created everything and who is unchanging in all of His attributes. He is today as He was yesterday and how He will be tomorrow. This God sounds like someone we would want as an advocate, doesn't it?

Even more is the fact that this God has chosen to be our "shepherd." Consider for a moment that the God of whom Scripture records that "the earth sees and trembles and the mountains melt like wax before" (Psalm 97:4-5) and in which we sing "the mountains bow down and the seas will roar at the sound of His name" is the same LORD David writes of as his shepherd. Isn't that amazing? Think of the contrast. In David's day, shepherding didn't rank very high on the most-desired career list. In fact, for families who kept sheep, it was a job reserved for the youngest son. Shepherds lived with their sheep 24/7. No matter the conditions, it was expected the sheep would be fed, guided, and protected. Not an easy task when you consider that sheep were not very intelligent and required a great deal of attention. Sheep were also prone to wander off. If the LORD is our shepherd, guess who we are? We're the sheep. We are not always as smart as we think we are, and we're certainly prone to wander.

So from the opening verse of this psalm all the way through its end, David gives testimony to the faithfulness of the LORD as He guided him throughout his life. All of Psalm 23 should comfort us greatly as we encounter life's circumstances. But if Psalm 23 consisted only of this one verse, it would be enough. To know that the LORD, the great "I AM" chose to be our shepherd is amazing. I hope you sense His love. What's more, in John 10, Jesus says, "I am the good shepherd … the good shepherd lays down his life for the sheep … I give them eternal life, and they will never perish and no one will snatch them out of my hand." In everything and in every way Christ, our Shepherd is sufficient to meet every need we have. He will guide you wherever life happens to take you. As it was with David, let that be a matter of great comfort for you today.

Prayer

LORD, thank You for choosing to be my shepherd, not just a shepherd but my shepherd. I know I am prone to wander; forgive me for that. Help me to stay close to You, recognizing that You willingly laid down Your life for me. Give me comfort and peace, knowing You are sufficient to meet my every need. Amen!

Monday: Psalm 23:1-6
Tuesday: Psalm 121:1-8
Wednesday: Psalm 131:1-3
Thursday: Ezekiel 34:1-31
Friday: John 10:11-16, 10:27-29; Hebrews 13:20-21

Week 21

The Priority Relationship

If anyone comes to me and does not hate his own father and mother and wife and children and brothers and sisters, he cannot be my disciple.
—Luke 14:26

I'm sure you love your family. I would venture to say you would do anything in your power to help them in any way. I certainly love mine and would do the same. That is the Christian way. This gospel we proclaim should be lived out. The call to love others and deny ourselves is straight from God's Word, so could Jesus have really been serious when He said, "If anyone comes to me and does not hate his own father and mother and wife and children and brothers and sisters, he cannot be my disciple" (Luke 14:26)? You didn't read that wrong. He was completely serious.

When reading this section of Luke and its teaching on discipleship, verse 27 gets most of the attention: "Whoever does not bear his own cross and come after me cannot be my disciple." It should get attention because it's true that as Christians, we are called to set aside our self will and follow Christ. We are all called to be disciples. Disciple means "learner," and Scripture doesn't allow for a distinction to be made between being disciples and Christians. When Jesus gave the Great Commission, he didn't say, "Go therefore and make Christians," he said, "Go therefore and make disciples" (Matthew 28:19-20). We must not think of discipleship as some higher level of Christianity—it is Christianity.

When we think of Jesus, our tendency is to focus on His love for us, and we should, but sometimes when we do, we end up redefining His expectations of what our priorities should be. Our Lord has called us to place our loyalty to Him before all else. Jesus set a very direct standard: "If anyone comes to me and does not hate …" In this verse, "hate" means only to love less. As many of us seek to be of help to those we love, we end up hurting the One who loves us the most. We accept that denying ourselves is a call from Christ, but somehow we put the call to serve others in a misplaced position. Though our intentions may be noble, it is still wrong because it keeps us from doing what the Lord would have us do.

Have you allowed yourself to fall into thinking that it's okay to serve someone's need, even if just temporarily, at the expense of obedience to the Lord, saying, "He'll understand"? In his devotional *My Utmost for His Highest*,

Oswald Chambers writes that for those who truly love the Lord, obedience is a delight and doesn't cost that person anything, and even though our obedience will cost and inconvenience others, it's a cost we have to let be paid. He continues by saying, "We can disobey God if we choose and it may bring immediate relief to the situation, but it will grieve our Lord. However, if we obey God, He will care for those who have suffered the consequences of our obedience. We must simply obey and leave all the consequences with him." He then concludes with a warning: "Beware of the inclination to dictate to God what consequences you would allow as a condition of your obedience to Him."

You see, the key to our relationships with others is not found in a self-help book, this devotional, or a visit to a psychologist, though they all may be helpful. The key is in keeping our priorities in order and making our relationship with Christ our first priority at all times and in every measure. Jesus expects and deserves nothing less. It is only when you and I, by the power of the Holy Spirit have committed ourselves to prioritize our relationship with Jesus that all our other relationships can be what God would have them to be. I hope you believe that. Our God is gracious and loving, but He is also a jealous God, jealous of anything we let take priority over Him, even the good things. It is biblical to love our spouses, parents, children, and siblings less than we love the Lord. It's when we do it intentionally that we will actually love them more because we now have the ability to see them, not as we once did, but how our Lord does.

Prayer

Lord, help me be committed to loving and obeying You before anything or anyone else. There are many things, even good things that compete with You for my attention. Help me keep You as my first priority. You demand and deserve nothing less. As I rely on the power of Your Holy Spirit to be obedient, the great result is that I will love others as You would have me to love them. By this, may You be glorified!

Monday: Luke 14:25-33
Tuesday: Luke 9:23-27, 9:57-62
Wednesday: Matthew 8:18-22
Thursday: Matthew 10:34-39
Friday: John 12:25-26

Week 22

Just Do It

Be doers of the word, and not hearers only, deceiving yourselves.
—James 1:22

Like so much of Scripture, many consider James 1:22 optional, but it's not. It is a command: "Be doers of the word, and not hearers only, deceiving yourselves" (James 1:22). Also translated as "prove yourselves" and "do not merely listen," James' concern as he wrote this letter was that the Jewish Christians spread throughout the Mediterranean region had reduced their faith to just acknowledging a set of facts about Jesus. He called this faith "dead." As he continued writing, he compared the different responses to God's Word, likening them to looking in a mirror.

Metaphorically speaking, God's Word is like a mirror. When we look at His Word, we see ourselves as we truly are. The people who are "hearers and not doers" are those who, though they may have looked intently into the mirror, seem to have forgotten what they saw. What might have happened? Did they not like what it was they saw? Maybe they got distracted by other things they thought were more important. Whatever the case, they forgot. Now contrast that with the people who are not only hearers but "doers who act." These are people who look at God's Word with a heartfelt desire to discover its deepest meanings, eager to make application for life.

Are you just acknowledging facts about Jesus, or is your faith "living"? How satisfied we can sometimes be to go to church on Sunday and leave without thinking God desires any change in our lives. Though we may not say it out loud, our attitude can be, *Well, I went to church, and now I'm off to the rest of my week.* In this age of relativism, we then take comfort in comparing ourselves to those who didn't even take time to go to church at all. Don't be satisfied by measuring your faith and obedience relative to other people. Measure your faith by what God's standard is. Be a "doer" and not a "hearer" only. Former pastor of The Moody Church in Chicago and Bible teacher, Warren Wiersbe says, "Too many Christians mark their Bibles, but their Bibles never mark them." Let God's Word mark your life today. When you and I "hear" and do not act, we are only deceiving, or as the Greek renders, "cheating" ourselves.

A few verses later, James says the "doer who acts will be blessed in his doing" (James 1:25). Don't cheat yourself out of that blessing. A heart truly open to hear God's Word is a heart that desires to obey and apply God's Word. Whatever God maybe speaking to you about right now, take the advice James gives us in this letter and "just do it."

Prayer

Lord, thank You that Your Word makes demands on my life.
Don't let me be deceived. Search my heart for the things I need to change,
things You want me to do, or perhaps things You do not want me to do.
Through Your Spirit, help me be a "doer" of
Your Word and not a "hearer" only.

Monday: James 1:19-27
Tuesday: Matthews 7:21-27
Wednesday: Luke 6:46-49; John 13:12-17
Thursday: Luke 11:27-28; Romans 2:13; James 2:14-20
Friday: 1 John 2:1-6

Week 23

The Perfect Builder

Unless the LORD builds the house,
those who build it labor in vain.
—Psalm 127:1

The current economic situation in the United States is as difficult as it has been in years. It has impacted the business community as well as many families. One of the hardest hit areas in this downturn has been home and property values. Additionally, jobs have been lost; many who are employed are in fact underemployed and unable to keep up with the standard of living they were accustomed to. As a result, many families are at risk of, among other things, foreclosure of their homes. Over a lifetime, many have labored to build a life for their families. Part of that building process likely included the purchase of a home.

As we've built our lives, specifically our homes, what have we used to build them? Who is it we've relied on to build our families? There are many homes, whether for financial reasons or not, at risk of foreclosure—that is, spiritual foreclosure. The question is why?

"Unless the LORD builds the house, those who build it labor in vain ..." (Psalm 127:1) Solomon, known for his wisdom and as the king who built the temple in Jerusalem is the author of Psalm 127. Though it might appear to have been written for the occasion of building the temple, such is not the case. The specific reason for which this psalm was written is unknown. When considering the last few verses, it is evident this psalm is more than about building physical structures only, it's about building families as well.

Where does the LORD fit in as you set the priorities in your house? Is He first? Husband, wife, father, mother, son, daughter, brother, sister, do you take seriously the guidance from the Lord as He directs your life, or do you just fit Him in when it's convenient? Like the church, each part of the family functions as part of a whole. Father and mother, husband and wife; you set the tone for the priorities in the home. Has the LORD built your house, or have you contracted its building out to other things? Though they may be noble things, if they've taken the place of the LORD, you have built your house in vain.

Former pastor and Bible teacher, Warren Weirsbe says, "Strong families begin with strong marriages, a man and a woman who love each other and want to live for each other and both for the Lord. Anything less than that is less than God's will." Husband, do you love your wife as Christ loves the church (Ephesians 5:25)? Wife, are you the "crown" of your husband (Proverbs 12:4)? Son, daughter, brother, and sister, God has given you responsibility as well. Do you honor your father and mother (Exodus 20:12, Deuteronomy 5:16)? If our families are to be what the LORD would have them be, each member must earnestly seek His guidance. Though the pace may be different for each family member, the direction should be the same. If you have built your house with things that won't last and it stands at risk of spiritual foreclosure, there's good news. God owns the bank and stands ready to forgive your debt because Jesus has paid it in full. So, if never before and forevermore, let the LORD build your house.

Prayer

Lord, forgive us for our failures. Build me, LORD, and build my house that we will serve You faithfully each day. Thank You for Your never-ending grace. Watch over our families and strengthen us to follow You with grateful and humble hearts. Thank You for Jesus Christ, who paid my debt, not with money but by the cross. He is worthy of my honor.

Monday: Psalm 127:1-5
Tuesday: Deuteronomy 6:4-9
Wednesday: Ephesians 5:22-33
Thursday: Ephesians 6:1-4; Exodus 20:12; Deuteronomy 5:16
Friday: Ephesians 6:10-18

Week 24

Polluted Offerings

How have we despised Your name?
—Malachi 1:6

At the point of Malachi's prophesy, one hundred years had passed since the Jewish exiles return from captivity at the hands of the Babylonians. Their return resulted from the overthrow of the Babylonians at the hands of the Persians. Though at this time they were still under foreign control, the people of Israel were well established in their homeland. Persian rule allowed greater autonomy for Israel. By now, the temple in Jerusalem had been rebuilt and Jewish priests were functioning in the temple and sacrifices were being offered to God. For all practical purposes, there was nothing that hindered the people's religious expression.

Malachi is the last book in the Old Testament before four hundred years of silence. In it God delivered a message of judgment to Israel, not only to the people at large but to the priests as well. Their problem was their attitude and God condemned it. Malachi uses what is known as a disputational style of prophesy, a question-and-answer method in which an original charge is made by the prophet, followed by a cynical response from the people who then objected to the charge, prompting the prophet to elaborate further on the charge. The primary purpose of the book of Malachi was to call Israel to renew their covenant faithfulness to the LORD.

James Montgomery Boice writes in his commentary on the book of Malachi that "more than any other Old Testament book, Malachi describes that modern attitude of mind that considers man superior to God and that has the audacity to attempt to bring God down to earth and measure him by the yardstick of human morality." Was the problem Boice described in the quote above simply a problem of Israel during the days of Malachi or is it a problem that exists today? What are our attitudes as we make our offerings to God?

"How have we despised Your name?" (Malachi 1:6). This was how the priests responded upon hearing Malachi's charge that they have despised the name of the LORD. They should have been leading the Hebrew people, setting an example for them to follow, but instead, they were every bit as much a part of the problem. They showed a complete lack of respect and reverence for the LORD. Instead of offering unblemished animals as prescribed in the law, they sacrificed blind, lame, and sick animals. This passage speaks directly to the role and responsibility of those called to ministry, but it also carries an important application for every Christian.

Much like those in Malachi's day, all of us have in some way shown contempt toward God and then had the audacity to ask how so. All of our lives are an act of worship, and our attitude in worship matters. Have you rationalized your sin and then entered worship believing God doesn't care about that sin?

This was a crucial issue in Malachi's day, as the Old Testament sacrifices pointed to the perfect sacrifice of Jesus Christ. It is also a crucial issue today. Though we do not make the same offerings as the people in Malachi's time, we are called to bring our offerings before the Lord. It's not that He needs them, but He certainly deserves them. Our offering is ourselves. We are to be a "living sacrifice" (Romans 12:1a). Many times we fail in this endeavor. Thankfully, we have Jesus Christ, the perfect Lamb, who was sacrificed on our behalf. And because His sacrifice is perfect, not only are our polluted offerings of the past covered, but so are our present and future polluted ones. God's grace covers every sin. That's good news for all of us and our only proper response to His grace is that our offering be "holy and acceptable to God" (Romans 12:1b).

Prayer

Lord, there are so many times I have entered Your sanctuary with total disregard for Your holiness and then had the audacity to ask, "How have I despised Your name?" Forgive me for that sin and help me be an offering that is pleasing to You. Help me to never try to measure You by any human standards. Your Word tells me who You are. Thank You so much, God, that You have provided the perfect sacrifice, Jesus Christ, to pay for the polluted ones I have too often offered. Let me be a sacrifice that pleases You each day.

Monday: Malachi 1:6-2:9
Tuesday: Leviticus 22:17-33
Wednesday: Deuteronomy 15:19-23; Micah 6:6-8
Thursday: Hebrews 10:1-14
Friday: Romans 6:12-13, 12:1

Week 25

Turning the Other Cheek

To one who strikes you on the cheek, offer the other also.
—Luke 6:29

Why do we find it so easy to retaliate? What is it about human nature that makes us want to make sure the person who hurts us is hurt even more? Even if we don't act on it, we still wish it and that's every bit as bad in God's eyes. Nobody denies the difficulty in turning the other cheek, but that is exactly what Jesus taught. You may be thinking, *I know that somewhere in the Bible it says an eye for an eye.* And you would be right, but the Old Testament intent for "an eye for an eye" was that of proportional justice, the idea that no matter the social class, the punishment would fit the crime. But sinful people, as they often do, take the intent of a passage, use it out of context, and misrepresent it. Such was the case in the circumstance of the Old Testament references to "an eye for an eye" approach. It is and never was meant to be a license for payback.

Jesus said, "To one who strikes you on the cheek, offer the other also" (Luke 6:29). No, Jesus wasn't kidding! In fact, in the verses just prior, He said, "Love your enemies, do good to those who hate you, bless those who curse you, pray for those who abuse you" (Luke 6:27-28).

Today, as you go through your day and people strike you on the cheek, some lightly and some not so lightly, resist the temptation to retaliate. To love your enemies is a command. To turn the other cheek is a command. But most importantly is who it is that gave the command. He is the one who expressed love for His enemies and a willingness to be humiliated by turning the other cheek like no other. His name is Jesus.

Prayer

Thank You, heavenly Father for Your Word. I confess my failure to take Your Word seriously on this issue. Forgive me and help me do what is unnatural in my own strength to do. Help me to please You and love those who strike out at me. After all, You loved me first. Amen.

Monday: Luke 6:27-36
Tuesday: Leviticus 24:17-23
Wednesday: Matthew 5:38-48; Romans 12:14-21
Thursday: Matthew 26:57-68
Friday: John 18:19-24

Week 26

Weightless

Let us also lay aside every weight, and sin which clings so closely, and let us run with endurance the race that is set before us.
—Hebrews 12:1

When you see the word *therefore* in Scripture, don't overlook it, because it's an important word. It is important because it directs you to what the writer has previously said. Since Hebrews 12 begins with "therefore," we first need to consider the previous chapter. Hebrews 11 gives examples of people from the Old Testament who demonstrated their faith in the promises of God. Though the author of Hebrews is unknown, its purpose and recipients are not. This letter was written to both Jewish Christians and non-Christians in hopes they might see the supremacy of Jesus Christ above both angelic beings and the Mosaic law. The Hebrew writer describes Jesus as the great High Priest, better than the Old Testament mediators and sacrificial system whose "once for all" sacrifice accomplished salvation. The latter part of Hebrews then calls the Jewish people to respond in faith and to endure as they live out that faith. We are called to do the same.

"Therefore, since we are surrounded by so great a cloud of witnesses, let us also lay aside every weight and sin which clings so closely, and let us run with endurance the race that is set before us" (Hebrews 12:1). The "cloud of witnesses" are those persons mentioned in chapter 11 who demonstrated their faith and who even now are spectators of our lives. When considering the primary purpose of Hebrews and that its recipients were believers and unbelievers, the writer appears to be referencing two different things when he writes that they are to "lay aside every weight and sin." The "sin" to be put away was unbelief. The "weight" the Jewish community was to "lay aside" was legalism. Jewish Christians struggled to let go of the old religious regulations they thought would earn God's favor.

Way too often, we believe there are certain things we have to do to earn God's favor. As a Christian, you have already earned His favor in salvation. As an unbeliever, salvation comes freely by God's grace through Jesus Christ alone. You can't earn it. Our believing we have to do something in order for God to love us more insults the grace He bestows. We are, however, to consider our response to that grace and put aside those modern day "weights," those things that take up time and energy and would have us settle for less than the very best, a relationship with our Savior. These "weights" keep us from finding what God would have us find in our relationship with Him—true joy and contentment. They also hinder our living for His glory. As Christians, that should be our daily goal—to live for the glory of Christ. Admittedly, it's difficult and the truth is, left to ourselves, we can't do it. But Jesus, the founder of our faith has made us "perfect" before the Father. Let us fix our eyes on Him. Will you do that? I hope you will because as long as you remain weighed down, you will always be settling for less than the best, less than what God desires for you, but most of all, less than what He deserves.

Prayer

Lord, there is so much for us to be weighed down with in this world. Often is the case that I allow these things to take Your place. When I do, not only am I not giving You the glory You deserve, I am cheating myself. Forgive me, God, and through Your Holy Spirit help me seek my joy and contentment in my relationship with You. Thank You for Christ, who paid my sin debt. Now let me "lay aside" anything that would hinder that relationship.

Monday: Hebrews 11:1-31
Tuesday: Hebrews 11:32-12:2
Wednesday: Hebrews 12:3-29
Thursday: Ephesians 4:17-24; 1 John 2:15-17
Friday: 1 Corinthians 9:24-27; 2 Timothy 4:6-8

Week 27

Are You a Hindrance to the Lord?

Get behind me, Satan!
—Matthew 16:23

How often do we sit consoling that family member or friend concerning a particular circumstance in his or her life in hopes of providing good counsel? As Christians we should listen, be supportive, and provide godly counsel to others, but how many times do we come back with the words, "I understand" and "that's not fair"? The truth is sometimes it may be hard to understand, and sometimes it may not be fair. But on the other hand, don't believe agreement and empathy always equal good advice and true love. The intent is not to discount good advice and loving support but to warn about allowing for self-pity as God is sovereignly working in the life of someone you care about. Jesus would have none of that.

Was there any disciple closer to Jesus than Peter? Did you know that in every listing of the twelve apostles, Peter is always listed first? Peter was part of Jesus' "inner circle" of disciples who was present on certain special occasions. So when Jesus began to tell His disciples that He must go to Jerusalem and suffer death, only to be raised, Peter reprimanded Him, "Far be it from you, Lord! This shall never happen to you" (Matthew 16:22). What do you think Jesus said in response? "Yeah, I know, it really isn't fair, thanks for caring, Peter"? Hardly. In fact, Jesus responded quite the contrary to what Peter expected, saying, "Get behind me, Satan! You are a hindrance to me" (Matthew 16:23).

Try to picture the look on Peter's face and imagine what he might have been thinking after he heard Jesus' response. "I thought Jesus said it was me on which He would build the church. After all, I'm the one who recognized Him as Messiah." Just prior to verse 23, Matthew records what Jesus said after Peter declared him to be the Christ: "And I tell you, you are Peter, and on this rock I will build my church, and the gates of hell shall not prevail against it" (Matthew 16:18). Christ of course is the rock, and in a sense the apostles played a foundational role in building the church. Peter loved Jesus, and I'm sure his intentions were noble, but in this case Peter was a "stumbling block," failing to see that Jesus' death on a cross was all part of the plan.

How often does your well intentioned advice go against the will of God? How often does your advice or listening ear allow for self-pity? No one knows the circumstance of your family member or friend better than the Lord. Nor does anyone love them more.

Nineteenth century English pastor, Charles Haddon Spurgeon, once said, "Even when you can't trace God's hand, you can always trust His heart." Just as Jesus' death was God's sovereign plan, He has also allowed that circumstance to come into the life of that someone you care about. We may not know what the Lord is doing, but He is at work. We just need to be there for those we love to testify of God's goodness and help them trust His purposes. Sometimes we think we are helping when we are actually hindering, allowing others to wallow in self-pity while the whole time God is working His perfect plan. As you listen and give advice, be careful not to be a frustration to what God has purposed to show or teach someone else. As you listen, is your mind set on the things of God, or is your advice based on the "things of man"? As you listen, set your mind on the things of God that you may be used by Him in the lives of others. After all, our heavenly Father knows best!

Prayer

Lord, let my advice never be a hindrance to Your will. I know Your will cannot be frustrated by man, but help me seek Your will first. I know You work sovereignly in the lives of people in good times and difficult times. Help me to be on guard against self-pity in my own life and to give godly counsel to others. You are good and Your plan is perfect because You are perfect.

Monday: Matthew 16:13-23; Mark 8:31-33
Tuesday: Genesis 3:1-6; Matthew 4:8-10
Wednesday: Matthew 10:2; Mark 3:16; Luke 6:14; Acts 1:13
Thursday: Matthew 17:1-13, 26:36-46; Mark 9:2, 14:32-33; Luke 9:28
Friday: Romans 14:13-18

Week 28

The Lie about Grace and Sin

What shall we say then? Are we to continue in
sin that grace may abound?
—Romans 6:1

If you answered yes to Paul's rhetorical question posed in Romans 6:1, you need to consider where you are in your relationship with Christ. You may even need to consider if you have one. It's doubtful any of us would admit to it if asked out loud, but ask yourself, "Do I rely on God's grace in order to do something I know I shouldn't, saying God will be gracious"? That is different than relying on God's grace when you do something that you shouldn't. It is a difference of the heart. We are all human and we are all sinful, but we should never use that as justification to ignore God's call for us to be holy (Leviticus 11:44, 1 Peter 1:16). It may seem as if I'm splitting hairs on this point, but consider that in Paul's day, some posed this very question to him as he preached. Paul preached that the Jews were not under the law but under grace. This brought criticism that his message led to people continuing in their sin and the accusation that his preaching was wrong.

God's grace has always been used as an excuse to sin. Jews bound to the Mosaic Law were critical of Paul for what he preached. Others mistook his preaching to mean that God's grace excused their sin. Paul addressed this by asking, "What shall we say then? Are we to continue in sin that grace may abound?" (Romans 6:1). He then answered it very directly: "By no means!" (Romans 6:2). It's worth repeating, though in a little different way a point made earlier. It is one thing to understand sin as a reality yet quite another to sin and excuse it by God's grace. The theological word that describes this is *antinomianism*, which means to deny that what God's law teaches in Scripture should control the life of the believer. Those who would ascribe to this belief would say that provided a person continues to believe, his or her behavior makes no difference regarding salvation. It's the idea that one can accept Jesus Christ as Savior but not Lord. Scripture doesn't teach this possibility. It teaches that Jesus is both Lord and Savior (Romans 10:9).

In his book *The Gospel According to Jesus*, John MacArthur says, "Any message that presents a savior who is less than Lord of all cannot claim to be the gospel according to Jesus. He is Lord, and those who refuse Him as Lord cannot use Him as Savior." MacArthur goes on to say that those who reject His reign amounts to nothing more than a futile attempt to hold on to sin with one hand while taking Jesus with other.

Those who have as a pattern of their lives deliberate and willful sin, saying, "My God will be gracious," are not saved. Many Christians, however, have found certain areas in which they have refused to submit to the lordship of Christ. God desires there be no area of our lives in which submission is less than complete. We must never presume upon His grace. God is gracious, but grace properly understood and received creates a desire in our hearts to please Him. Obedience is no longer a burden but a pleasure. The Bible teaches that it's impossible to be "in Christ" and accept sin as a way of life. That it is possible is the lie. Don't believe the lie and thereby corrupt the biblical view of grace.

Prayer

Lord, thank You for Your grace. My salvation is possible only because of it and only possible because Jesus Christ earned it for me. Help me recognize and appropriately apply the grace You have shown in all areas of my life. Grace is never an excuse to sin, so convict me when I act as if it is. Let my desire be to please You in everything I do. Amen!

Monday: Romans 6:1-23
Tuesday: 1 Peter 1:13-16; Galatians 5:13-26
Wednesday: 1 Corinthians 6:1-20
Thursday: 1 Peter 2:1-25
Friday: 1 John 3:1-10

Week 29

Marks of a Faithful Teacher

For Ezra had set his heart to study the law of the LORD,
and to do it and to teach his statutes and rules.
—Ezra 7:10

Most of us have heard the phrase, "Do as I say, not as I do." Maybe you've used it yourself. How much credibility would someone have as a leader if he or she said those words to you? I imagine not very much. It's critical a person be a reflection of what it is he or she advocates.

Ezra was a good example of such a person. He was a Jewish priest in the line of Aaron and a scribe who returned to Israel from Babylonian captivity in 458 BC. Scribes were uniquely skilled in the law of Moses, and as such, Ezra was given authority by the Persian king to initiate a set of reforms designed to lead Israel to repent of their sins, and to return to covenant faithfulness they had sworn before the LORD. The hand of God was on Ezra as he stressed to the people of Israel the need for the Scriptures to guide their lives (Ezra 7:9).

"For Ezra had set his heart to study the Law of the LORD, and to do it and to teach his statutes and rules …" (Ezra 7:10) Ezra had a mission given to him by God, a mission to teach. In this verse we are given a very important pattern that serves a useful purpose for each of us even today. By the way, whatever you do, don't make the mistake in thinking that just because you may not serve in an official "teaching" capacity, this passage does not apply. What Ezra patterns in his life as it relates to the Scriptures every Christian should do.

The English Standard Version of the Bible says Ezra "set his heart" on what God prepared him to do, other translations use the word *devoted*. Whatever version used, the implication is that Ezra himself was steadfast and ready to do what God called him to do. He studied the law, and as this verse indicates, taught its "statutes and rules."

Both studying and teaching are enormously important, but I want to highlight another aspect of what characterized Ezra's role as a priest and scribe. He lived what he taught. What kind of credibility do you believe Ezra would have had when initiating his religious reforms if he had said to the people of Israel, "Just do as I say, not as I do?"

Friend, parent, Sunday school teacher, or pastor, are you living what you are teaching? Is your heart set to do the will of God in your own life first, before teaching others? Do not ever underestimate this very fact because with the great responsibility that comes with teaching also comes a greater expectation by God (James 3:1). Yes, it is true we no longer live under the Mosaic law but under grace, but God's grace properly understood should lead us to desire in our hearts to do His will. God honors the teaching of the one who sets his heart to study, to do, and to teach. In whatever capacity you serve, be found a faithful teacher.

Prayer

Lord, I thank You for all the faithful teachers who have followed the pattern that Ezra gives us in Your Word. I pray I would be found faithful in my teaching capacity, to whatever extent that may be. You call all of us to know You and to proclaim You to others. Let Your Holy Spirit help me set my heart to study Your Word, do what it calls me to do, and teach it to others. Let me be found faithful. Amen.

Monday: Ezra 7:1-8:36
Tuesday: Nehemiah 8:1-9:38
Wednesday: Nehemiah 10:1-39
Thursday: Malachi 2:1-9; 1 Timothy 4:6-16
Friday: - 1 Matthew 5:17-19; 7:24-27; James 1:19-25

Week 30

Character, Prayer, and the Power of God

Thus says the LORD ... "I have heard your prayer; I have seen your tears. Behold, I will heal you.
—2 Kings 20:5

The LORD hears the prayer of the righteous (Proverbs 15:29). Hezekiah is a testimony to this biblical truth. Hezekiah reigned as king of Judah for twenty-nine years. The northern kingdom of Israel had fallen to the Assyrians in 722 BC, and now only the southern kingdom of Judah survived. Unlike his father, Ahaz, Hezekiah was a man who had an abiding trust in the LORD in every situation. In fact, it is written about him, "He did what was right in the eyes of the LORD" (2 Kings 18:3). During his reign, Hezekiah set about reforming worship in Judah to what it should be, taking an even stronger stand than some of his predecessors who also sought the LORD's will. Though he had an abiding trust in God didn't mean that Hezekiah wasn't in need of some reassuring along the way, particularly as it related to the Assyrian threat. The prophet Isaiah provided that reassurance. The Assyrians failed to take control of the southern kingdom as they had the northern kingdom. God proved faithful to the trust Hezekiah placed in Him, but the story of Hezekiah also provides another powerful lesson for us.

In chapter 20 of 2 Kings, the story of Hezekiah's life threatening illness and recovery is told. When the prophet Isaiah told him to get his house in order because he was going to die, through his tears Hezekiah prayed, reminding the LORD of his faithfulness and how he had done good in His sight. "Thus says the LORD ... I have heard your prayers; I have seen your tears" (2 Kings 20:5a).

As mentioned above, Scripture gives testimony that a righteous life opens up the LORD's ears to prayer. Sin hinders our prayers. Many fail to appreciate this as we go to God in prayer. Hezekiah had a pattern to his life; a pattern that honored God and sought His guidance. God honored this prayer. Through the prophet Isaiah, the LORD told Hezekiah that He had seen his tears, but the LORD also saw something else. He saw his life, and

Hezekiah's life matched his prayer. There is great power in the prayers of righteous people. "Behold, I will heal you" (2 Kings 20:5b) Though Scripture doesn't indicate that Hezekiah specifically prayed for healing, only that he not die, the LORD healed him.

Be thankful God has healed us from our most significant illness: sin that leads to death. Though we can never completely know God's plans and purposes, His healing of Hezekiah should encourage us as we go to God in prayer for healing because He has the power to heal. We don't have to be perfect for God to answer our prayers. If we did, He wouldn't answer anyone's, but how we live our lives does affect our prayers.

Hezekiah followed the LORD with his "whole heart." He lived with a desire to please the Him. Will you do the same? When you pray, do you not desire that your prayers have maximum effect? If so, then live like Hezekiah—not perfect, but always with a desire to please the LORD in all things. Remember, "The eyes of the LORD are on the righteous, and His ears are open to their prayer" (1 Peter 3:12). Are His ears open to yours?

Prayer

Father, thank You that we can come before You in prayer knowing that You hear them. Your power is certainly enough to answer any prayer. With the power of the Holy Spirit, let my life be led in such a way that it would please You to open Your ears to my prayers. Amen!

Monday: 2 Kings 18:1-37
Tuesday: 2 Kings 19:1-37
Wednesday: 2 Kings 20:1-11
Thursday: Psalm 39:1-13
Friday: 1 Peter 3:10-12; James 5:13-16

Week 31

A Clean Vessel

Now in a great house there are not only vessels of gold and silver but also of wood and clay, some for honorable use, some for dishonorable use.
—2 Timothy 2:20

Heart disease is the leading cause of death in the United States. The most common form is coronary artery disease in which plaque builds up in the arteries, eventually causing them to narrow. When this happens it restricts blood flow and subsequent oxygen to the heart. If left untreated, coronary artery disease will often lead to a heart attack. Essentially, what has happened in people with coronary artery disease is that the artery or blood vessel's usefulness has been diminished, no longer able to fulfill its intended purpose for the heart. God also has an intended purpose for His people.

"Now in a great house there are not only vessels of gold and silver but also of wood and clay, some for honorable use, some for dishonorable use" (2 Timothy 2:20). The word *vessel* is used in various contexts throughout Scripture. In Romans 9, Paul uses it in his teaching on divine sovereignty in salvation. He uses it in 2 Timothy 2:20 to illustrate the faithfulness, or lack thereof, of Christians. Paul wrote Timothy, telling him there were honorable vessels, those made of gold and silver, but there were also dishonorable vessels made of wood and clay. His mention of the "great house" at the beginning of verse 20 is a reference to the believing church.

When coronary heart disease is diagnosed there are various treatment strategies a physician may employ to keep the vessel from narrowing again. They also make certain recommendations to the patient, the goal being to keep the vessel clean and useful in supplying needed oxygen to the heart. As Christians, our desire should always be to faithfully serve the Lord. Ultimately, we are cleansed only by the blood of Christ. But in the context of this verse, Paul says that in order to be used by God, one has to cleanse himself (or herself), meaning he needs to avoid those things, both doctrinally and morally that would hinder his good work. This is only possible by the continuing work of the Holy Spirit in our lives.

The truth Paul shared in his letter to Timothy is a truth that applies to all our lives. What we "are" matters. Perfect, no, but always on guard to ensure that the pattern of our lives is pure. We cannot believe God doesn't care about the things we do that don't bring Him honor and glory. God will not use a dishonorable vessel. His plans and purposes will still be accomplished; we will just have no part in it and thereby miss the blessing of having served Him.

Heart disease is treatable but incurable and always carries with it a greater risk of death. As a child of God, you have been raised from death to life because of what Jesus Christ has done for you. In response, ask yourself, *What kind of vessel do I want to be?*

Prayer

Dear God, thank You that You have cleansed me by the blood of Christ. My desire, Lord, is to be used to further Your kingdom. Help me be mindful of the need to remain pure and avoid things that would hinder my good work. My good work is not what saves me but is evidence of my salvation. I want to be a faithful and honorable vessel that You would be pleased to use. It is only possible by the power of the Holy Spirit. Father, I pray for that power each day. Amen.

Monday: 2 Timothy 2:14-26
Tuesday: Romans 9:1-33
Wednesday: 1 Corinthians 3:10-17
Thursday: 2 Corinthians 4:1-21
Friday: 1 Timothy 3:14-16

Week 32

Who Is like You?

Who is like You, O LORD, among the gods? Who is like You, majestic in holiness, awesome in glorious deeds, doing wonders?
—Exodus 15:11

Do you remember in chapter 3 of Exodus when the LORD called Moses from the burning bush? Do you remember how, when He told Moses He was sending him to Pharaoh and that Moses would lead Israel out of Egypt, Moses responded with a series of questions? They were really excuses. After an initial response of "Here I am" (Exodus 3:4), Moses soon realized the reality of what God was calling him to do, and he felt incapable. The LORD was gracious, and in spite of these excuses, He equipped and used Moses anyway.

Fast forward to Exodus 15, sometime after Moses reluctantly obeyed the LORD, telling Pharaoh to "Let my people go" (Exodus 5:1). Of course Pharaoh refused, and the LORD then brought on ten plagues, the tenth (death of the firstborn) finally resulting in the Egyptians sending the people of Israel out of their land. But Pharaoh changed his mind, and along with his army pursued Moses and all of Israel. Most of us probably know the story of when Israel crossed the Red Sea. As the Israelites saw the Egyptians in pursuit, they became fearful and said to Moses, "What have you done in bringing us out of Egypt?" (Exodus 14:11). Complaining and weak faith were characteristic of the Hebrew people. Sound familiar? But the LORD wasn't finished, and He told Moses to lift his staff, stretch out his hand over the sea, and divide it. When he did, the sea opened up, the people of Israel crossed, and the Egyptians followed. Israel successfully crossed the Red Sea. The Egyptians on the other hand incurred some difficulty. Convinced their battle was not really with Israel but with the LORD they panicked, but it was too late. When they turned to flee, Moses stretched out his hands again and the sea returned to normal, drowning the whole Egyptian army.

Throughout the book of Exodus, we see God sovereignly working in the lives of His people. He controlled everything, from the hardening of Pharaoh's heart in disallowing Israel's release to His power being displayed in the plagues to the crossing of the Red Sea. But why, you ask? It was so the

LORD would not only receive His due glory but would also be feared. "Who is like you, O LORD, among the gods? Who is like you, majestic in holiness, awesome in glorious deeds, doing wonders?" (Exodus 15:11). Moses knew the answer. No one is like the LORD!

There are a number of instances where God is praised for revealing His character, and in this particular instance, Moses' song was a celebration of the LORD demonstrating His power and rule over Pharaoh and the Egyptian army. The LORD was responsible for Israel's deliverance. Once welcomed in Egypt, as the Hebrew population grew they became a threat to Pharaoh, such a threat that he made them slaves to the Egyptians. After living in Egypt for 430 years, the LORD delivered Israel out of captivity, using Moses to lead the way.

How long were you "captive" before the LORD delivered you? The word *exodus* comes from a Greek expression meaning "a going out." A key theme of the book of Exodus is Israel's deliverance or their "going out" of Egypt.

Just as the LORD delivered Israel, He stands ready to deliver you. Our deliverer is Jesus Christ, and if you have trusted in Him alone, you are captive no longer. Praise Him for the wondrous deed He did in His life, death, and resurrection to deliver you. Praise Him for His power in saving your soul, the same power He uses to protect it. If you're still captive, trust in Christ alone and see His power in salvation that He will work for you this very day. There is no one like Him!

Prayer

LORD, You are a great God, like no other. Thank You that
You made a way for me to approach You. Jesus, thank You for being that
way and for delivering me from my sin, sin that deserved death and hell.
LORD, let me praise Your name, always mindful of Your wondrous deeds.
You are my deliverer! Amen!

Monday: Exodus 3:1-4:31
Tuesday: Exodus 12:33-13:22
Wednesday: Exodus 14:1-31
Thursday: Exodus 15:1-21
Friday: Psalm 106:1-48; Revelation 15:1-4

Week 33

Seek and Find

You will seek me and find me, when You seek me with all Your heart.
—Jeremiah 29:13

If you've done many word-search puzzles, more than likely you have found that in each puzzle there's one particular word that always seems to elude you. In fact, when you began, you most likely sought the words that were the easiest to find.

We have a God who never tries to hide but desires to be found by you and me. Our God desires a relationship with us, a relationship in which through our lives He is glorified. What are we seeking? It seems in this day and age we seek everything but God to satisfy us. Perhaps you believe there exists something in world that, when you finally find it, will give you that ultimate satisfaction you have been looking for. Maybe it's money, power, or prestige. It might be a relationship you've been desiring or a job you've been seeking. The words go like this: "That would make everything perfect." Don't believe it!

Jeremiah's ministry spanned five decades until he was forced from Judah. His prophesy paints a picture of sinful people in whom God's judgment would come. It came at the hands of the Babylonians. Though judgment and destruction of Israel occurred, Jeremiah also promised restoration for the people. Written shortly after the 597 BC deportation, this section of Jeremiah's letter to the Jewish exiles was meant to reassure them that God had not abandoned them.

Now, we must acknowledge that at this point in Israel's history, it looked as if He had, but through the prophet Jeremiah, God told the people, "I'm still here." It was God's judgment for their sin that had brought them to this place. Where has your sin taken you? Perhaps it has caused broken fellowship with other people. More importantly, maybe it has caused broken fellowship with God. It's doubtful any of us have ever encountered the type judgment Israel did as a result of our sin, but have you been or do you ever feel like God has sent you into some type of modern-day exile, estranged from the people and things closest to you? Maybe a time when it seemed you just couldn't find God?

It's worth repeating: our God desires to be found. "You will seek me and find me, when you seek me with all your heart" (Jeremiah 29:13). He's not hiding. He is not like that one word in every word-search puzzle that is so elusive. Just as genuine prayer would restore the people to their homeland, God will respond and restore you when you genuinely repent and pray for forgiveness. He will be found, but you must seek Him with all your heart.

In this verse, the heart symbolizes the totality of our being, both our wills and our emotions. This change of heart results in our loving God and is the essence of true saving faith. So, let me ask you, who gives us the faith and changes our heart so that we may seek and find God? Be careful not to take the credit here because the apostle Paul gives us the answer. The faith that saves, "it is a gift of God" (Ephesians 2:8). So, let me ask you one last question. Who really sought who?

Prayer

Lord, thank You for the gift of faith. Thank You for being a God who doesn't hide. Never let me think I can seek You on my own terms because the truth is, if left to me I would still be Your enemy. Thank You for seeking me and opening my heart to the words of truth. Whenever I drift, help me to humbly seek You that I may be restored to where You would have me be.

Monday: Jeremiah 29:1-23
Tuesday: Jeremiah 1:1-19, Deuteronomy 4:25-31
Wednesday: Deuteronomy 30:1-20; Proverbs 8:17; Isaiah 55:6
Thursday: Psalm 119:1-16
Friday: Psalm 119:57-72

Week 34

Am I a Pleasing Aroma?

For we are the aroma of Christ to God among those who are
being saved and among those who are perishing.
—2 Corinthians 2:15

Think of the smell of your favorite dish your mother or grandmother cooked. Now contrast that with the smell of a dish you really didn't like when it was being cooked. You knew that smell as well, and it probably wasn't very appealing to you. Whatever the aroma, it was either pleasing or not.

What do you "smell like" to Jesus? Corinth was one of the largest and most influential cities in the Roman world. It was famous for its commerce and its arts and crafts. But Corinth was also one of the most corrupt cities in the Roman world. It was so corrupt that the word *corinthianize*, which means to live an immoral life, was coined to describe it.

Paul founded the Corinthian church during his second missionary journey, spending eighteen months ministering there. The church at Corinth greatly confounded the apostle Paul. Upon his departure, the church began to sink back into the immoral behavior characteristic of the city itself (e.g., worship of other gods, disharmony among people, and sexual immorality). In other words, the church in Corinth didn't smell too good.

Paul wrote several letters to the Corinthians addressing numerous problems within the church. One purpose for which he wrote 2 Corinthians was to defend his ministry. "For we are the aroma of Christ to God among those who are being saved and among those who are perishing" (2 Corinthians 2:15). In this verse and the verses that surround it, Paul speaks of an "aroma." As you would expect, the Greek word for "aroma" has to do with a smell or an odor. In the Old Testament, when this word was used, it normally referred to a sacrifice pleasing to the LORD (Exodus 29:25, Leviticus 1:13). The sweet aroma of Christ, as the ultimate sacrifice, is an even fuller "aroma" than what was referenced in the Old Testament.

When Paul encountered Jesus on the road to Damascus, he was changed forever. His life's goal went from persecuting those who believed in Christ to proclaiming Him like no other. From that meeting on, Paul himself was what the Holy Spirit inspired him to write we should be a "living sacrifice" pleasing to the Lord. He was a pleasing aroma.

Though God delighted in Paul, as he ministered, sharing the gospel of Jesus Christ, he always had plenty of opposition. There were some people who didn't like Paul's "sweet aroma" and rejected his message about Christ. On the other hand, some were attracted by it and came to salvation as a result of the message he preached.

Has Jesus changed you like that? Are you a sweet aroma to Him? Does He delight in you? Let us be a sweet smell to Jesus.

Prayer

Lord, let me be like Paul. Let all my delight be in You, that You would be pleased. My desire is to be a "sweet aroma." I know it's only because of Jesus Christ, the ultimate sacrifice, that allows me to please You. Thank You for the grace and mercy through Him, and let my response be worthy of that sacrifice each day. Amen!

Monday: 2 Corinthians 1:1-24
Tuesday: 2 Corinthians 2:1-17
Wednesday: 2 Corinthians 4:1-6; Hebrews 13:1-19
Thursday: Romans 12:1-2; Ephesians 5:1-21
Friday: Philippians 4:10-20

Week 35

I Believe, But ...

I believe; help my unbelief!
—Mark 9:24

Jesus healed in many ways and under many different circumstances. He healed with a touch, with a word, and out of pity, and He even healed those who touched His clothing as He passed by. Jesus healed people in His presence but also those who were not. He healed some who did not even believe in Him, showing no faith at all, while on other occasions, Jesus chose to emphasize the power of faith in His healing.

Jesus' healing brought a lot of attention from people. Much like today, in Jesus' day, people loved it when He brought healing and blessing. Such was the case when Jesus healed the boy possessed by an evil spirit. When Jesus inquired about an argument taking place, the boy's father began to explain to Him about how an unclean spirit was affecting his son. He shared with Jesus that he had asked the disciples to cast out the unclean spirit, but they were unable. Jesus then expressed the faithlessness of not only the scribes but the disciples, saying, "O faithless generation, how long am I to be with you? How long am I to bear with you?" (Mark 9:19).

So what we find in this passage is a boy's father seeking the healing power of Jesus, while on the other hand, Jesus' primary interest was in having the father believe and to put his trust in Him. Jesus then said, "All things are possible for the one who believes" and immediately the father replied, "I believe; help my unbelief!" (Mark 9:24). Though it may have been weak, this statement suggests the faith of the boy's father.

Is that how our faith is at times—present but weak? There are two points to consider from this passage. First, don't believe that because you have times of doubt, you have no faith. Doubt is possible within faith. Even John the Baptist, who announced Jesus as the Christ, the one who would "take away the sin of the world" (John 1:29) sent his disciples to Jesus to inquire as to whether Jesus was really the One or should they look for another (Luke 7:19).

Secondly, don't use this passage as a crutch to make you think it's all right to persist in weak and stagnant faith. Yes, God accepts our weak faith, but at the same time, He expects there to be an upward trajectory in our faith and trust in Him. We should always be growing. Many Christians go through life powerless because instead of bringing their weak faith and putting it at the feet of the Lord, they remain in their unbelief or doubt in the power of God. They then use their human imperfection as an excuse for doing so.

In this passage we see how this father brought his weak faith before Jesus, expressing a desire to believe even more firmly. Jesus healed the boy in spite of that weakness. He will do that for us as well. God wants us to come with our needs, even when our faith is weak. His power is great. His healing hands are far reaching. Have faith in God; believe in Him even when it seems as if you can't. Bring your weak faith before Jesus and watch Him be faithful to supply your present need.

Prayer

Lord, I believe. Though all too often it is weak, my desire is to become stronger in my faith that Your power makes all things possible. Lord, we realize that in Your plans and purposes, healing in this life is not what always happens, but instead, sometimes the healing comes when we enter Your presence. Help me see with my faith instead of my eyes, knowing You heal and are the One who is always faithful. Amen!

Monday: Mark 9:14-29
Tuesday: Mark 6:53-56, 7:24-37
Wednesday: Mark 8:22-26, 10:46-52
Thursday: Luke 7:1-23
Friday: Luke 8:26-56

Week 36

Who Have I Sinned Against?

Against you, you only, have I sinned.
—Psalm 51:4

Oh, how it might be different if we saw sin the way David wrote about it in Psalm 51. Sometimes it took him a while to recognize his sin and who his sin offended, but David always got there.

Unfortunately, many of us never get to that point. All sin first and foremost is against God. Seen or unseen, known or unknown, God sees it and knows it. However, for some reason we have this idea that our "hidden" sins—hidden in the sense that few if any know about them, or are sins that don't necessarily affect anyone else—are somehow of less importance to God. You know the ones I'm talking about: the lie you told, that sexual indiscretion. How about that questionable tax deduction or that fake expense you submitted on your company expense report? How about that anger, even if only in your heart, toward your spouse, parent, or child? The list goes on and on.

"Against you, you only have I sinned ..." (Psalm 51:4) David likely wrote this psalm as a result of when he was exposed as an adulterer and murderer by Nathan the prophet (2 Samuel 12:1-14). Guilty of many sins in his life, this particular episode might have been David's worst by comparison, but that's the point. Comparisons are not what we should be making, but we do. Our tendency is to say, "He committed murder, he should be sorry for that." Somehow in our minds we look at sin and too often categorize them into "big sins" and "little sins," acting as if one is more of an insult to God than the other. By the way, as it relates to the issue of murder, remember what Jesus said: "You have heard it said ... you shall not murder; and whoever murders will be liable to judgment. But I say to you everyone who is angry with his brother will be liable to judgment" (Matthew 5:21-22). The point Jesus was making was that anger and hatred carry similar motives as murder, and the attitude one displays in their anger or hatred carries the same kind of guilt as the act of murder itself. You will not find anywhere in Scripture where Jesus ever minimized one sin relative to another.

Our Lord has set a high standard, and just as David did, you and I have broken that standard. As he came under conviction of sin, David repented and recognized that though he had sinned against others, more than anything or anyone else he had sinned against a holy God. Upon his repentance, David always found God ready to restore him.

If only we had the same attitude toward our sin. If only we could just realize that in our own lives and recognize that whether "big" or "small," all sin is an offense to God. What would happen in our lives, and in our relationships with others, if we had enough appreciation for our relationship with the Lord to be totally undone at how our sin affects Him? It wouldn't make our sins toward others less important but more important. How we relate to others is always dependant on how we relate to God and the view we have of Him. See Him as holy because He is.

We have a gracious God who has forgiven us much. He stands ready at all times to forgive and restore us to a right fellowship with Him. He has provided the means of that forgiveness in the person of Jesus Christ. So, as the Holy Spirit convicts you of your sin, don't make excuses, don't compare offenses as lesser or greater. Honor the work Christ did on your behalf and recognize your need to seek forgiveness—forgiveness of others, of course, but more than that, forgiveness of God.

Prayer

Father God, thank You that You forgive my sin. Thank You that
You gave us Your Son who lived a perfect life and died on the cross, only
to be raised that I may live. Help me to not try negotiating as to what type
of sin offends You the most because they all do. You are holy. Help me
recognize that while yes, I have sinned against others and I need to seek
their forgiveness, first and foremost I have sinned against You. Fill me
with Your Spirit that I would recognize this each day that I live. Amen!

Monday: Psalm 51:1-19
Tuesday: 2 Samuel 11:1-12:23
Wednesday: Psalm 25:1-22, 32:1-11
Thursday: Psalm 38:1-22, 130:1-8
Friday: Psalm 143:1-12; 1 John 1:8-9

Week 37

God Knew Me When

For You formed my inward parts; You knitted me together
in my mother's womb.
—Psalm 139:13

"Then God said, 'Let us make man in our image, after our likeness'" (Genesis 1:26). Is there really anything left to be said? I don't suppose we should expect those who do not believe in God or the creation account to accept the authority of Genesis 1:26, but we should expect more from ourselves. Psalm 139 is a powerful passage of Scripture that speaks to the issue of human life. Specifically, verse 13 speaks of God's involvement in the development of an unborn child. "In the beginning," Humanity began because of God, and of all that He created, His creation of man was the crowning jewel. Because God created everything, including humans, everything belongs to and is subject to Him. But of all that God created, His relationship to humans is a special one, as it is only human beings that bear His image.

"For you formed my inward parts; you knitted me together in my mother's womb" (Psalm 139:13). David recognized that God's interest in him came even before he was born. Psalm 139:13 is certainly not the only verse of Scripture that recognizes the personhood of a fetus. David also wrote, "I was brought forth in iniquity, and in sin did my mother conceive me" (Psalm 51:5). Luke records that John the Baptist, while still in his mother, Elizabeth's, womb "leaped for joy" when Mary greeted her (Luke 1:44). God said to Jeremiah, "Before I formed you in the womb I knew you, and before you were born I set you apart; I appointed you as a prophet to the nations" (Jeremiah 1:5).

God's activities in our lives don't just begin at birth. I know as Christians most of us realize that, but consider where the abortion debate has gone in recent years. While there are certainly Christians who have spoken out and held firmly to Scripture regarding this issue, others have not, allowing this debate to be parsed around the issue of rape or incest. Admittedly, these are difficult circumstances, but far more often, convenience is what dictates the decision to have an abortion. Since when does rape or incest change the authority and the truth of Genesis 1:26? It doesn't. Just because a child is conceived in sin doesn't change whether or not that child is made in the image of God. The unborn child deserves the same right to life as anyone else. Believe God can bring about "good" even in those things that we're incapable of seeing how anything "good" might come. God will bless our honoring Him on the matter of abortion. We just have to be willing to stand up and testify to the truth of His Word. If we as Christians refuse to, then who will? Our belief in the absolute authority of Scripture is a must. Not doing so only widens the divide between our will and God's. For those who have thought or think differently on this matter, like all sin, God's grace covers this one. Look to God's Word for clarity, and open your heart to His. His will is clear. And then ask yourself, *Do I want to be at odds with that?* I pray you will answer no.

Prayer

God, forgive our nation for the sin of abortion. Forgive us
individually when we think more of our comfort and reputation than
we do Your Word. Thank You, Father, that we have forgiveness in Jesus
Christ, forgiveness so great that it covers any sin. Your Word is clear
regarding the value You place on human life, even the most fragile human
life, the unborn. Help us to stand firm on Your truth each day, no matter
the consequence, and let our desire always be
to have our will conform to Yours.

Monday: Psalm 139:1-24
Tuesday: Psalm 71:5-6, 51:5
Wednesday: Jeremiah 1:4-5; Luke 1:39-45
Thursday: Job 10:9-12; Isaiah 44:2
Friday: Psalm 22:9-11; Isaiah 46:3

Week 38

Jesus' Death Ordained by God! How Can It Be?

This Jesus, delivered up according to the definite plan and foreknowledge of God, you crucified and killed by the hands of lawless men.
—Acts 2:23

Satan is a great manipulator. Under his influence, Judas and the Jewish religious leaders carried out exactly what they desired to do, kill Jesus. There should be no doubt they were responsible for their actions in that matter. As my pastor, Buddy Gray, preached from Luke 22:1-6, he referred to the words of the apostle Peter recorded by Luke in Acts 2:23: "This Jesus delivered up according to the definite plan and foreknowledge of God…" (Acts 2:23a). A point made during the sermon was that the death of Jesus Christ had been planned by God. Go ahead and ask, "Why would God do that?" As Peter preached at Pentecost, he affirmed God's sovereignty over events in the world—in this case, specifically the crucifixion and death of Jesus Christ. The word *foreknow* means more than just to know beforehand, it means to choose beforehand. To be completely clear, God ordained the crucifixion of Jesus Christ. Does that absolve Judas and the Jewish religious leaders of their responsibility? No!

"…you crucified and killed by the hands of lawless men" (Acts 2:23b). Peter didn't hesitate placing the responsibility for Jesus' crucifixion exactly where it belonged, with those "lawless men." He didn't say, "These men can't be blamed, God made them do it." The Bible teaches that although God allows evil to occur in order to accomplish His purposes, He is never responsible for it. It's not for you or me to fully know how God's sovereignty works out in world events, but it is for us to know He is sovereign as it does.

So why would God ordain the death of Jesus Christ? As Buddy made the second and final point in his message about Jesus' death being planned by God, he preceded it with a few fitting attributes of God. He said the death of Jesus Christ was planned by a holy, loving, and gracious God. "It was the will of the LORD to crush him" (Isaiah 53:10).

God is holy, loving, and gracious, and He did what He did for that reason. God loves us so much that He sent His Son to die. Jesus loves us so much He willingly died. As He prayed to the Father in the garden of Gethsemane, facing the pain and hurt of separation from the Father, He said, "not my will, but yours be done" (Luke 22:42).

Jesus completed the work the Father gave Him to do. He went to the cross. Of course Judas played his part, Herod and Pontius Pilate played theirs, and certainly Satan played his, but the director of it all was God, as nothing that happened occurred outside His sovereign hand. Though it may be hard to understand, accept that not only does what God ordained and Jesus accomplished show the extent of their love for us, but more than that, it results in His glory. What a great God and Savior we have!

Prayer

God, You are sovereign and You are good. Your ways are often beyond our ability to comprehend them, but they are always perfect. Help me trust in that sovereignty even when I can't fit all the pieces together. Thank You for the love You showed even in the evil act perpetrated by evil men. This is how You chose to bring salvation, and I thank You for that salvation. Help me live my life worthy of the gift of Your Son.

Monday: Acts 2:14-41, 3:13-18, 4:27-28; Isaiah 53:10-12
Tuesday: Matthew 26:1-16, 26:47-68, 27:1, 27:11-26
Wednesday: Mark 14:1-11, 14:43-50, 15:1-15
Thursday: Luke 22:1-6, 22:47-53, 22:66-23:25
Friday: John 13:21-30, 18:1-14, 18:28-19:16

Week 39

Discipleship Lived Out

What you heard from me in the presence of many witnesses entrust to
faithful men who will be able to teach others also.
—2 Timothy 2:2

Jesus commanded in Matthew 28:19-20, "Go therefore and make disciples of all nations, baptizing them in the name of the Father and of the Son and of the Holy Spirit, teaching them to observe all that I have commanded you." Known as the Great Commission, this is not meant for a few but for all Christians.

The apostle Paul lived the Great Commission. For twenty years, he ministered alongside Timothy, a young man who joined him during the second missionary journey. When Paul wrote 2 Timothy, his last letter, he knew his death would come soon. Knowing that, he chose to write to Timothy. Naturally, he had a number of things on his mind, but the primary purpose for writing Timothy was to encourage him as he carried on the faithful ministry of the gospel. Paul knew the truth of the gospel was under attack.

"What you have heard from me in the presence of many witnesses entrust to faithful men who will be able to teach others also" (2 Timothy 2:2). After twenty years, there was very little Timothy didn't know and had not seen Paul live out in his own life. Paul's message to Timothy was to take those lessons he had learned from him and pass them on to other faithful men who would fight to preserve the truth of the gospel. What you testified to in this passage is Paul living out discipleship. Paul battled for the truth in many ways; he was a committed evangelist, missionary, pastor, and church planter, but Paul was also committed to discipleship as evidenced by his relationship with Timothy. The word *disciple* means learner and is characterized by one faithful person teaching another.

The truth attacked in Paul's day is also under attack today. Discipleship is a means God uses to protect truth, but unfortunately it is greatly lacking in the church today. This is evidenced by the church's weakness in standing up to cultural changes that conflict with what God has made clear in His Word.

James Montgomery Boice says a fatal defect in the church is the lack of a true commitment to discipleship. He believes one of the reasons for problems in the church is a defective theology that "separates faith from discipleship and grace from obedience." Boice concludes by saying, "Discipleship is not some supposed second step in Christianity, as if one first became a believer in Jesus and then, if he chooses a disciple." Obviously, in order for discipleship to be what it should be, our theology must be correct. Paul's of course was and therefore his writings, as well as the writings of others, and his life serve as an appropriate model for each of us.

More importantly, Jesus calls us to discipleship. Are you a disciple? Are you learning from a man or woman who is more mature in the Christian faith to help you grow in your walk with the Lord? Are you leading men or women in discipleship? If not, will you commit to? This is what all Christians are called to do, so, "Go therefore …"

Prayer

Lord, help me this day to make time and commit to what Your Word calls me to do. You have called all Christians to discipleship, yet I often act as if You have only called some. Convict me when I am disobedient and help me to live out this command. Give me the desire to seek out others more mature than me to learn from and to seek out those less mature to teach. God, this is Your will. Help me do it.

Monday: 2 Timothy 2:1-26
Tuesday: Matthew 16:24-28, 28:16-20
Wednesday: Luke 9:23-27, 14:25-33
Thursday: Acts 16:1-5; 2 Timothy 3:10-17
Friday: John 8:31; John 13:35

Week 40

Training Them to Go

Train a child in the way he should go; even when he is old
he will not depart from it.
—Proverbs 22:6

Like other parents, I love my children and want to fulfill every one of their dreams. The problem with doing that is it sometimes conflicts with what they truly need. There are situations that arise where a difficult decision has to be made. Though your child hasn't necessarily done anything wrong, sometimes what you have to do or the decision you need to make seems like punishment to them, and maybe to you as well.

This is where we as parents have the potential to fall into several traps. Our society will always see the best way forward differently than our Lord does. The Lord's standards are set much higher than society's, and too often we follow society's. Sometimes sheer convenience alone will set a trap for you. Then there will be times you just don't want the conflict and you'll take the easier but wrong road. I'm sure most of us as parents try to properly balance fulfilling the desires of our children with teaching them godly principles to serve them throughout their lives. At times in my own experience as a parent, I'm not sure how good a job I've done at that. There have been times our culture has exerted a greater influence on me than I would prefer.

These are appropriate questions to consider as a Christian parent. What is having the greatest influence on you as you prepare your children to go out on their own? Is it our culture or is it our God?

"Train up a child in the way he should go …" (Proverbs 22:6a) To "train" is to dedicate or initiate in pointing your children in a life direction and moral conduct that pleases the LORD. King Solomon is credited with having a primary role in the wisdom movement, writing many of the proverbs. When the LORD appeared to him in a dream and asked what He could give him, Solomon requested wisdom. "Give your servant therefore an understanding mind … that I may discern" (1 Kings 3:9). Solomon's request is the intention of the book of Proverbs, to instill wisdom—but not wisdom by worldly standards but by God's.

Proverbs is an intensely practical book that addresses many areas of life. Training our children in the ways of the LORD requires love but also instruction and discipline. We distort the true definition of love when we think instruction and discipline are not included in it. "…even when he is old he will not depart from it" (Proverbs 22:6b). Proverbs are not necessarily promises but general principles for life. As a parent, you may do everything right and godly and your children may still stray. Just don't let that possibility cause you to neglect both the need and God's call to properly train them. You already have the manual for the training. It's God's Word. All the distractions and influences around us make this type of training a challenge; however, it is imperative we get it right. Pray for grace daily.

And when your children go, pray that with the Lord's help they will have learned some of the lessons you and I were faithful to teach.

Prayer

Lord, there are many lessons I need to teach my children,
and there are many methods to use to prepare them for this world. Help
me through Your Spirit to train them according to Your will given us in
Your Word. I know there will be many challenges, traps, and distractions,
but help me keep my focus on You that I may teach my children Your
ways, for they are perfect. I pray, Lord, that You will grant our children
grace and that in their lives they will not only practice these lessons but
teach them to their children as well. Thank You, Lord, for hearing this
prayer. Amen.

Monday: Proverbs 22:6, 22:15, 13:24; Psalm 78:1-8
Tuesday: Deuteronomy 4:1-14
Wednesday: Deuteronomy 6:4-8, 11:1-32
Thursday: Joshua 24:1-15
Friday: Ephesians 6:1-4

Week 41

Denying the Savior

He said, "I am not."
—John 18:17

There was so much, you might say, "meat" in this passage. The application drawn was piercing but at the same time encouraging. As I heard the sermon on John 18:15-27 unfold, I was struck at the end of verse 17. "He said, 'I am not'" (John 18:7). This was the first of Peter's three denials of Jesus. Jesus predicted this would happen, but Peter refused to believe Him. Pretty typical of Peter, I suppose; he was kind of prone to getting ahead of himself every now and then. He once said that though all the other disciples would fall way, he wouldn't. He also told Jesus, "You shall never wash my feet." This was not a humble response to Jesus' intention but a prideful one. How about when he rebuked Jesus after He foretold of His death and resurrection? Peter was ripe for his denial we now consider. Peter's denial of Jesus was probably his greatest humiliation and is told not only in the gospel of John but all the gospels.

How would you like for your most humiliating moments to be recorded for the entire world to see? Peter's first recorded denial was in response to a servant girl who kept watch at the door into the court of the high priest. You might think if Peter was going to wilt under pressure, it would at least be in front of one of the religious or political leaders. But Peter wasn't immune to failure of this magnitude and neither are we.

All of us have denied Jesus in some form or fashion, hiding our allegiance to Him simply because it seemed out of step given the particular circumstance. Jesus, however, is different. He never fails and is always faithful. When He was confronted by Jewish leaders, specifically the high priest, Jesus did not waver one bit from the truth of His teaching, "I have spoken openly to the world. I have always taught in synagogues and in the temple, where all Jews come together. I have said nothing in secret" (John 18:20). When He uttered these words, He was struck but again never wavered.

Peter's first denial was followed by two more, and upon the third, the rooster immediately crowed (John 18:25, 27). In his gospel Luke provides a little more detail surrounding these events. He recorded that just as the rooster had crowed, as Jesus was being taken from place to place, He turned and looked at Peter. It was then Peter recalled that Jesus had predicted this very moment. Peter left in tears. Here we have a failure of the greatest magnitude. Peter wasn't just some low-level disciple. Remember how Jesus had changed his name and proclaimed that on Peter, the "rock," He would build His church? Some kind of rock, you might say.

Have you failed your Savior that way? Have you denied Jesus in the most trivial circumstances in front of your own "servant girl"? Though Jesus didn't look you directly in the eye as He did Peter, He saw your denial. I mentioned that this passage carried application that was both piercing and encouraging. You might ask, "How can this passage be encouraging?" As you ponder this question, let me ask you, what did these denials by Peter hold for his future, and what do our denials hold for ours? Here's a hint: the answer is found in Jesus Christ. To be continued …

Prayer

Lord, thank You that when I fail, You never do. Keep me strong and dedicated to Your cause, knowing I can trust You. My desire is to never deny You in any circumstance or situation. It is only through the filling of the Holy Spirit in my life that I can accomplish that. Fill me!

Monday: John 13:36-38
Tuesday: John 18:1-27
Wednesday: Matthew 26:30-35, 26:47-75
Thursday: Mark 14:26-31, 14:66-72
Friday: Luke 22:31-34, 22:47-62

Week 42

Jesus Restores

Lord, You know everything; You know that I love You.
—John 21:17

God has a plan and purpose for each of us. When Jesus called Peter to be one of His disciples, it was not so He could evaluate his performance relative to the other disciples and then determine what that purpose would be. Jesus' purpose for Peter had long been planned. So here we are, after the resurrection and some three years removed from when Peter obeyed Jesus' call to follow Him, when the events described in this passage occur.

After being told the stone had been taken away from the tomb, Peter investigated. He went into the tomb only to find the linen cloths lying there. John records that Peter and the disciple with him didn't fully understand the Scriptures concerning Jesus' resurrection. Peter returned home and resumed his occupation as a fisherman, his occupation prior to Jesus' call. What do you believe was Peter's lasting memory at this point in his life? Could it have been the look Jesus gave him after he had denied him the third time (Luke 22:60)?

"Lord, You know everything; You know that I love you" (John 21:17) were Peter's first words after Jesus asked him for the third time, "Do you love me?" Why do you think Jesus asked Peter this question three times? Perhaps to remind him of the three times he had denied Him? But each time Jesus asked this question and heard Peter affirm his love for Him, He provided him direction. Jesus said to Peter, "Feed my lambs," "Tend my sheep," and "Feed my sheep." These directions were so Peter would understand what would be his role and responsibility to the church of Jesus Christ.

At Pentecost and throughout the rest of his life, we see that responsibility demonstrated in Peter's life. He proved to be a worthy under-shepherd to Jesus, the chief Shepherd (1 Peter 5:4). But even at this point in John 21, Peter knew Jesus knew his heart and how much he loved Him. That love would eventually find Peter on his own cross. Tradition holds that like Jesus, Peter was crucified and that at his request, he was crucified upside down because he felt unworthy to die in the same manner as his Savior.

It may seem somewhat strange to find Peter's failures encouraging, but it shouldn't. Peter's faith never failed and the reason why was because it was

God who gave him that faith in the first place. He was the same Peter that Jesus proclaimed as a "rock" on whom He would build the church (Matthew 16:16). What failed Peter was self, and self is what fails you and me as well. Take heart and be encouraged that as God restored Peter and continued what He began in his life, He knows your heart as well and stands ready to restore you. No matter your failures, your denials, or your lack of courage in a given moment, Jesus says, "Follow me." So, follow Him!

Prayer

Lord, my restoration is only made possible by Your resurrection. You lived perfectly, You died willfully, and You conquered the cross on the third day. My, how this served to see You glorified through the life of Peter. When I fail You, Lord, restore me to a right fellowship. Help me live a life that glorifies You each day. Amen!

Monday: John 20:1-10
Tuesday: John 21:1-19
Wednesday: Matthew 16:13-20
Thursday: Acts 2:14-41
Friday: John 2:23-25

Week 43

The Lie about Grace and Knowledge

But grow in the grace and knowledge of our Lord and
Savior Jesus Christ.
—2 Peter 3:18

Nowhere does Scripture imply that God's grace frees us to remain ignorant concerning knowledge of our Savior. Grace should never be used as an excuse for laziness. As a redeemed child of God, our desire should be to grow in the knowledge of our Lord and Savior, Jesus Christ. The process by which we grow in Christ-likeness is called *sanctification*. Sanctification means to "set apart." There is, however, a progressive aspect to the sanctification process that doesn't end in this lifetime. This is not to say we are saved over time, only that our spiritual maturity is a lifelong process. Salvation occurs in a moment. Though sanctification is an act of grace, in no way should we be passive in the process. Instead we are to put forth human effort. This effort is enabled by the power of the Holy Spirit and has love for Christ as its singular motive. The idea is that we get to know Christ, not that in some way we have been forced to know Him. Knowing Christ is a privilege.

Scripture teaches that a believer is justified by grace alone through faith alone in Christ alone. It seems, however, at least to some degree the Protestant church has diminished anything that gives even the appearance of having a "works" aspect to it. I don't necessarily believe this is always the intention, but I sense it is the case. Think about that special someone you love. Remember when you first met him or her, how much you wanted to know about this person, how you studied his or her likes, dislikes, and desires? You just couldn't be knowledgeable enough. I imagine you did this for the purpose of knowing and subsequently pleasing this person more and more. Having this type of knowledge about someone also carries the advantage of minimizing the opportunity for anything to come between that relationship.

Why should the Lord expect any less from us in our relationship with Him? Part of the purpose Peter wrote this letter was to warn Christians of the false teachers trying to lead followers astray. While it was not possible to lose their salvation, Peter wanted to avoid having them affected by the erroneous teaching. He told them not to "lose your own stability" but to "grow in grace and knowledge of our Lord and Savior, Jesus Christ" (2 Peter 3:18).

This world offers many lies that require Christian discernment. Oftentimes the lie is mostly true, but it's still a lie. Don't fall for the lie that implies the doctrine of sanctification; growing in spiritual maturity spurs thoughts of legalism because humans put forth effort in this process. Those who make this claim are often those who don't want to submit to the lordship of Christ. God reveals Himself most clearly to us in His Word, and it is through this means, empowered by the Holy Spirit, that we grow in our knowledge of Christ. God's goal is that we be mature. Christian maturity is a shield that protects us from being carried away by false doctrine. This is important as we live in a world that increasingly denies Jesus Christ. But most of all, spiritual maturity brings God glory because it helps you live more in line with how He intended. And glory is what He deserves for giving us life through His Son, Jesus Christ.

Prayer

Jesus, I love You and I know You love me because You hung on the cross for my sin. Why would it even occur to me that You wouldn't want me to grow in my relationship and fellowship with You? Your grace doesn't excuse my ignorance but should instead create a desire in me to know You more. Knowing You and discerning Your will protects me in a world that denies You, helping me to live in a manner worthy of what You have done. Thank You, Lord!

Monday: 2 Peter 3:1-18
Tuesday: 2 Peter 1:3-11; 1 Peter 2:2; Ephesians 4:11-16
Wednesday: Colossians 1:9-14; 2 Thessalonians 1:3-4
Thursday: 2 Corinthians 4:1-6
Friday: Ephesians 1:15-23; Philippians 3:7-11

Week 44

Sola Fide (by Faith Alone)

The righteous shall live by faith.
—Romans 1:17

When October 31 rolls around most people automatically think of Halloween, but this day is a significant day in the life of the Protestant church. It is Reformation Day. It was on this day in 1517 that Martin Luther nailed his Ninety-Five Theses on the door at the church in Wittenberg, Germany. Luther was a catholic priest, and these Ninety-Five Theses were in effect his stated objections, primarily to the selling of indulgences (essentially the selling of salvation) by the Catholic Church, thus beginning a long period of conflict with the Church. "Unless I am convinced by Scripture and plain reason, I do not accept the authority of the popes and councils, for they have contradicted each other. My conscience is captive to the Word of God. I cannot and will not recant anything for to go against conscience is neither right nor safe. God help me. Amen." These were the words of Martin Luther in 1521, when he was called to recant his previous statements against the church. Much happened prior to this public confrontation between Martin Luther and the pope, and the Protestant Reformation that Luther led continues to have a tremendous impact today.

Reformation theology is built on what are called the five *solas*, a Latin word that means "alone." They are as follows: *sola Scriptura* (Scripture alone), *sola gratia* (grace alone), *solus Christus* (Christ alone), *soli Deo gloria* (the glory of God alone), and *sola fide* (by faith alone). Proper appreciation of these doctrines continues to be critical for the church today. As Luther studied the Scriptures, the Holy Spirit illuminated him to these precious truths and one in particular: "The righteous shall live by faith" (Romans 1:17).

The Bible tells us our righteousness comes through faith alone and is given as a free gift from God (Ephesians 2:8). Some denominations dispute this, and many Christians live as if salvation is by faith plus something else. Do you? What the Holy Spirit through the Scriptures showed Martin Luther was a person's right standing (righteousness and justification) before God had gotten lost in the Church. Scripture taught that salvation came by grace through faith in Christ, a stark contradiction to where the Church was at that moment and where many churches remain today.

This leads to another important point regarding faith, the object of our faith. Faith for faith's sake doesn't save, only faith in Jesus Christ alone saves. Though knowledge is indispensable to our faith, it is not that we just agree intellectually to what Scripture says about Christ. It is knowledge that leads to conviction and personal trust. Oftentimes we live as if our right standing before God is faith plus something else (you fill in the blank). Don't do that. Jesus Christ went to the cross so you and I wouldn't have to, and this gift of faith that He gives you and me requires no other payment. *Sola fide!*

Prayer

God, I am so thankful that by Your grace You have given me the gift of faith. Help me to never think or act as if I can do anything to earn salvation. I don't have to because Your gift is perfect because my Savior is perfect. Thank You, Jesus, for all You've done. Let me live a life of faith and rely on You in every way.

Monday: Romans 1:1-17
Tuesday: Habakkuk 1:12-2:5; Galatians 3:1-14
Wednesday: Ephesians 2:1-9; Hebrews 10:38-39; Philippians 3:1-11
Thursday: Romans 4:1-25
Friday: Hebrews 11:1-40

Week 45

Close Enough to Hear

But the LORD was not in the wind ... not in the earthquake ... not in the fire ... and after the fire the sound of a low whisper. And when Elijah heard it.
—1 Kings 19:11-13

It's not always a major event or an obvious moving of the Holy Spirit in our lives that the LORD uses to get our attention. Sometimes it is just a whisper. With good intentions, do you ever say, "When God desires for me to do something, He will show me and I'll obey"? Don't be so sure. Now, that's not to say you will not obey, and it's not to say God doesn't make His will so obvious that it becomes completely clear. The point is God does not only show us He is working in large and obvious ways, but that He also works in small and subtle ways. The question for consideration is less about how God chooses to reveal Himself to us and more about whether we are prepared to hear Him when He speaks.

Elijah was a faithful prophet. God called Elijah to oppose pagan worship and the influence it had on the nation of Israel. Worship of Baal, the storm god who provided the necessary rain for crops was widespread in the days of Elijah. During this time, Ahab was the king of Israel. Ahab was an evil king, but he also had an evil wife, Jezebel. She was perhaps a greater threat than the king himself. In 1 Kings 17-18, we are told of a severe drought that occurred in the land, a drought brought about as judgment for Israel, led by Ahab, forsaking worship of the true God for worship of Baal. As God would end this drought and the resultant famine in the land, it had to be made clear that it was He who was responsible for it. He used Elijah for this purpose. Elijah confronted, challenged, and defeated the prophets of Baal on Mount Carmel. True to His promise, the LORD sent rain. After this defeat of the prophets of Baal, Jezebel became enraged and threatened to kill Elijah. Coming off such a great victory from the LORD, why should Elijah be afraid? But he was and he fled, eventually ending up at Mount Sinai. "But the LORD was not in the wind ... not in the earthquake ... not in the fire ... and after the fire the sound of a low whisper. And when Elijah heard it" (1 Kings 19:11-13).

The LORD works and speaks in spectacular ways. Wind, earthquakes, and fire all symbolize God's presence in these ways, but in this particular case, He chose a different way, a whisper, to speak to Elijah and help him with his discouragement over Jezebel's threats. It would seem the LORD's acts on Mount Carmel would have been enough to cease any lingering rebellion? So, it was in a quiet way that the LORD chose to let Elijah know He was still at work.

It may be in that same quiet way the LORD chooses to communicate with you. Sometimes it's hard to perceive the LORD silently working out circumstances in our lives, but a better question is, are we really prepared to hear Him? When He speaks softly to us, will other interests or lesser commitments "making noise" in our lives drown out His voice? There are times God's desires for you will be crystal clear, but sometimes they may not be. So whatever manner in which the LORD works, the point is, He works. It takes a receptive heart to create a perceptive ear to hear His voice. Is your heart receptive to His speaking? Will you hear Him?

Though a momentary lapse of trust in the LORD, Elijah was indeed a faithful prophet. Will you be faithful? Will you search God's Word daily to discern His will? It is not up to you to determine the manner in which God will make His desires known. It may be in a spectacular way or it may be in a subtle, quiet way. In whichever manner the LORD chooses, we have one responsibility, an opportunity really, and that is to have put ourselves in a position to hear Him when He speaks. This can be done daily, as we seek Him in His Word. As you think about this, ask yourself, "Am I close enough to hear?"

Prayer

Lord, thank You for always being at work, be it a spectacular way or in a quiet way. I know it's through Your power that we accomplish anything pleasing to You. Thank You for giving us Your Word. Give me the desire to search it so that I may be close enough to hear You when You call, that I may do Your will.

Monday: 1 Kings 17:1-18:46
Tuesday: 1 Kings 19:1-20:43
Wednesday: 1 Kings 21:1-22:40
Thursday: 2 Kings 1:1-2:14
Friday: Matthew 17:1-8; Mark 9:2-8; Luke 9:28-36; James 5:13-18

Week 46

Always Listening

I love the LORD because He has heard ...
because He inclined his ear to me.
—Psalm 116:1-2

When I was young, there were times I spoke to my parents wondering if they were truly listening. As a parent, I realize that I do the very same thing I suspected my parents of doing. As a father, I may be there but not really present—hearing but not really listening. I guess that's just human nature. Thankfully, our heavenly Father is not like that.

Psalm 116 falls within a collection of psalms sung by the Jewish people, praising the LORD for His delivering them from Egypt. Though the author, date, and occasion of the psalm is unknown, the writer clearly faced a life-threatening event in which he needed deliverance. Considered a psalm of thanksgiving, the Israelite writer expresses gratitude to the LORD for saving his life in a time of great need. "I love the LORD because he has heard ... because he inclined his ear to me ..." (Psalm 116:1-2). The LORD heard the psalmist voice as he pleaded for mercy. More than just hearing, the LORD "inclined his ear."

Although God does not have a physical body, in this verse, as well as others, Scripture uses various parts of the body to describe God's activities. This is known as anthropomorphic language, defined in Wayne Grudem's *Systematic Theology* as language that speaks of God in human terms. Maybe more than you wanted to know, but helpful nonetheless. To "incline" indicates an even more personal touch than to simply just hear. The psalmist was amazed by the fact that the LORD would "incline his ear," but why? Was it that there was no one else willing to listen to his plea? Was he, like most of us, a poor listener? The psalm doesn't answer these questions, but it gives an indication as to the kind of God we have. He is a God who is incapable of being distracted such that He can't hear our pleas for mercy. He is able to help in any given situation; in fact, He desires to hear our cries for His help. But too often, you and I fail to turn to Him, believing we can handle it ourselves, or perhaps believing there are more important things the LORD has to deal with. Nothing could be further from the truth.

Often we are so easily distracted by our own selfish agenda that we neglect to give attention to those we love the most. Not the case with the LORD. He loves and delights in His children. My pastor always says, "The most important thing about you is your concept of God." Your concept of God matters if you are to fully appreciate the truth of this passage. The LORD, who has "inclined his ear" to you and me is the same LORD who, with His mouth spoke the world into existence. What a great God! Note how the psalmist responds. As a result of the LORD's faithfulness to hear his prayer and to deliver him from trouble, the psalmist became resolute in his response. He determines to continue to pray to, rest in, walk with, and worship the LORD. As our LORD has heard your prayers and delivered you, how will you respond?

Prayer

LORD, thank You that You inclined Your ear to hear my prayers. Thank You for Your Son, Jesus Christ, for without Him I
could have no relationship with You. I'm amazed when I think about the fact that You created everything and can still love me so intimately. Help me to never let that amazement cease. Thank You that You are not like we are: frustrated by circumstances, faithless in trials, and selfish in our service to others. Help me hear You each day and grow more and more in faithfulness to You.

Monday: Psalm 116:1-19, 17:1-15
Tuesday: Psalm 18:1-6, 31:1-24
Wednesday: Psalm 118:1-7, 40:1-3
Thursday: Psalm 55:1-23
Friday: Psalm 86:1-17

Week 47

One Way to Battle Sin

I have stored up Your word in my heart,
that I might not sin against You.
—Psalm 119:11

Temptation is not sin. Jesus was tempted, and we know He never sinned. The same cannot be said for you and me. Though we are sinners, our desire as Christians should be to not sin, and we should diligently fight against it every moment of every day. One way to do that is through spiritual discipline. There are many useful disciplines the Holy Spirit uses in our lives, but this verse suggests the discipline of Scripture memorization as one way to battle sin. "I have stored your word in my heart ..." (Psalm 119:11a). To "store," or as some Bibles translate "hide," is the idea of treasuring something greatly, seeing it as highly valuable.

Think of the various items we store and the purposes for which we store them. Some people store food in their freezer. What about storing furniture, tax files, medical records, etc.? The common rationale for putting something in storage is it may be useful at a later time. Such is the case for storing God's Word in our heart. In Scripture, "heart" is more than just the organ used to pump blood throughout our body. When we store God's Word in our heart, it is to internalize it. It is where our mind, will, and emotions agree.

You might ask, "Why do I need to store God's Word in my heart?" " ...that I might not sin against you" (Psalm 119:11b) Sin is anything that separates us from God. God knows we are sinful, but He hates our sin. Let me challenge you in case you're thinking Scripture memory is impossible. If you are, it's probably not memory you are lacking but the discipline to do it. Let me ask you, is your freezer full? Today we fill our minds with so much that doesn't serve any edifying purpose in our Christian lives. What useless things have you allowed to fill your mind that has crowded out God? Fill your mind with God's Word, and trust that the Holy Spirit will help you to recall it when it is needed. Why wouldn't He?

Also, let your motive be to please the Lord. This is one way to battle sin; there are others. Satan would desire us not take God seriously on this point. He'd prefer we ignore Scripture altogether. When we do, we can be sure he will win many battles.

Fortunately, Jesus has won the war. When Jesus was tempted by Satan in the wilderness He used Scripture to help Him face this temptation (Matthew 4:3). If God, who became man, saw fit to use Scripture to face temptation, who are you and I to think we don't need to? Store all the earthly things you may need, but make sure to store the most useful thing you can store, because chances are you will soon need it.

Prayer

Lord, I pray You would give me the desire to know Your Word and to memorize Your Word so that I might not sin against You. My mind is so cluttered with things that are useless and my attitude is often negative toward anything that requires much effort on my part. Clear my mind of those things that are useless so I can fill it with Your Word. Give me an attitude and a heart that desires to put effort into being able to recall Your Word. I don't want to sin, Lord, and I pray that the Holy Spirit will help me as I battle each day against sin. All for Your glory!

Monday: Psalm 119:9-16
Tuesday: Psalm 1:1-6
Wednesday: Psalm 19:1-14
Thursday: Psalm 37:21-31
Friday: Matthew 4:1-11; Luke 4:1-13

Week 48

A Tough Test Given by a Faithful God

Do not lay your hand on the boy or do anything to harm him.
—Genesis 22:12

" …Do not lay your hand on the boy or do anything to harm him" (Genesis 22:12) If you didn't know this story, you might think the person to whom this quote was attributed was a police officer, maybe a superhero in a movie, or perhaps a parent. It could be you don't know this story, but the fact that the reference is the book of Genesis, you know it comes from the Bible. Imagine for a minute that you knew nothing about this story, and then let's say I told you the one who spoke the words of this verse, in essence, the one doing the rescuing, was the same one who was responsible for the boy being in harm's way in the first place. What would you think? Well, the one who spoke these words was the LORD, and He said them to the boy's father, whom He had told earlier to sacrifice his son. This is the story of when the LORD told Abraham to sacrifice his son Isaac.

I believe if asked, most parents would say they would be willing to die for their child. I believe Abraham would have died for Isaac, but that's not what the LORD asked him to do. Instead, He asked Abraham to kill Isaac. I can't even imagine being asked by anyone, much less by God, to do this very thing to one of my children. If you're curious as to how this might bring God glory it is okay, but be cautious in closing off your mind and heart to God's ways and purposes. They are always greater than ours.

This story is really less about Isaac, the son, than it is about Abraham, the father. The LORD made a covenant with Abraham, promising to bless him and make him the father of a multitude of nations (Genesis 17:4). It was through Abraham's son, Isaac, that his offspring would be named (Genesis 17:19). For Abraham, this was a test to see if he was willing to give up his greatest treasure, because there was an even greater one, the LORD Himself.

God demands He be our greatest treasure, and He allows tests of faith in each of our lives—not so much that He can learn more about us but so we can learn more about Him. The LORD always proves trustworthy and

He did in this case, as He provided a ram as an offering to take Isaac's place at just the right moment. In his life, Abraham experienced the LORD's trustworthiness and faithfulness time and again, but make no mistake, on this occasion, though unsure of how it may end, he was prepared to carry out exactly what the LORD told him to do. That is walking by faith; the kind of faith that not only the LORD recognized but which the Hebrew writer recognized as well (Hebrews 11:17-19).

Certainly the LORD is not going to test you in the same manner He did Abraham, but He will test you. In these times of testing, will you do what God says even when it is contrary to everything you see and feel? Do you trust Him enough to obey?

More than Isaac and even Abraham, this story is about our LORD. We have a great God, so great in fact that not only did He provide the substitute for Isaac on that day, some two thousand years later He provided one for you and me. That substitute is Jesus, and on the cross at Calvary, God, who chose to rescue Abraham's son, refused to rescue His own.

Scripture says, "It was the will of the LORD to crush him" (Isaiah 53:10). And there you have Jesus, the perfect and sinless substitute who was willing to be crushed because our sin is that great, but His love greater. Because Jesus is perfect, our sin requires no further sacrifice. Our LORD is trustworthy and He always provides. We just need to walk by faith and trust in His promises, because unlike us, He always keeps His.

Prayer

Lord, thank You for the testimony of Abraham and his example
of faithfulness. He wasn't perfect, nor am I, but his heart was set to do
Your will. Let mine be also. Thank You for being trustworthy and faithful.
Thank You for giving me Your Son, Jesus Christ, the perfect sacrifice for
sin. So perfect that no other sacrifice will ever
be required. My, what grace!

Monday: Genesis 15:1-21
Tuesday: Genesis 16:1-16
Wednesday: Genesis 17:1-27
Thursday: Genesis 21:1-34
Friday: Genesis 22:1-19

Week 49

What If There Was no Resurrection?

That he was raised on the third day in accordance with the Scriptures.
—1 Corinthians 15:4

Our appreciation for something is often greatest when we consider the consequence of it never having been. There are people who don't believe in the resurrection because they don't believe in Jesus Christ. There are also those who have a misperception about why He came and who He claimed to be. This was also true in the apostle Paul's day. Paul was always concerned about the integrity of the gospel, emphasizing that the gospel he preached was that which he received from Christ. Of all the teaching in Scripture on the resurrection, 1 Corinthians 15 is the most comprehensive. In this passage, Paul mentions three elements of the gospel: Christ's death for our sins, His burial, and His resurrection on the third day. All of these elements are critical to Christ's redemptive work, but His resurrection is what we consider here. Think for a moment where we would be without it.

" …that he was raised on the third day in accordance with the Scriptures" (1 Corinthians 15:4). In this chapter of 1 Corinthians mentioned above, Paul tells us the consequences of there being no resurrection. He says that if there is no resurrection of the dead, then not even Christ has been raised. And if Christ has not been raised, then preaching is in vain, faith is in vain, God is misrepresented, sin is not dealt with, and all who have died "in Christ" have perished. He goes on to say that if it is only in this life that we hope in Christ then, "we are the most to be pitied" (1 Corinthians 15:12-19). Translation: If it is only in this life that we have hope in Christ, stay home on Sunday, throw away your Bible, and live as you please because we're hoping in something that isn't real. Our hope in eternity is built on the resurrection, and without it there is no reason for hope. But there is reason for our hope. There is reason because the Bible tells us Jesus was raised from the dead (1 Corinthians 15:20).

In church today, the resurrection is the least alluded to aspect of Christ's saving work. I'm not sure why that is. Maybe we just take it for granted? The resurrection is a necessary pillar of the Christian faith, and its affirmation has everything to do with not only salvation and justification but also biblical authority. It is often said that Jesus conquered sin on the cross, and I know what people mean when they say that, but His death alone is incomplete without His resurrection, as this is how we are justified before God (Romans 4:25). The victory was completed when Jesus rolled away the stone and came out of the tomb.

Though as a church we may only formally celebrate the resurrection once a year, as Christians we testify to it every Sunday and can live it each day. As you consider and celebrate all that Christ has done, make sure to thank Him for the resurrection, for because of it you will never suffer the consequence of it never having been. But even more, thank Him for the resurrection because it confirms God accomplishing His plan, and because of that, we have hope—hope in this life and for eternity. What a great God and Savior!

Prayer

God, I thank You for all of Jesus' work in His life and death
to save me. My sin is that great. But God, today I thank especially for His
resurrection, for if that didn't happen, I would be pitied and left without
hope. But I have hope, all because of You. Help me trust Your Word as I
live my life and as I testify about all of Jesus' redeeming work. You are a
great God and Savior!

Monday: 1 Corinthians 15:1-58
Tuesday: Matthew 16:21, 17:22-23, 20:17-19
Wednesday: Luke 20:27-40
Thursday: John 11:1-57
Friday: Luke 23:1-24:53

Week 50

Calamity in His Will

I am the LORD, who does all these things.
—Isaiah 45:7

"I form light and create darkness, I make well-being and create calamity."
These are the words of Isaiah 45:7, which precede the portion of the verse that
serves as our title. "I am the LORD, who does all these things" (Isaiah 45:7).
Perhaps we're indifferent to the LORD forming light and creating darkness.
I'm sure most of us love that the LORD makes well-being. However, when
it comes to creating calamity, some will say, "That can't be my God. My God
wouldn't do that. What happened certainly wasn't part of His plan."

A "calamity" is defined as an event that results in terrible loss, lasting
distress, and severe affliction. Two events that stand out as calamities in
American history are 9/11 and Hurricane Katrina. Why did these tragedies,
or for that matter, why does any tragedy happen? Scripture teaches that God
judges sin, but it's not for us to say whether or not it was sin He was judging
in either of these events. What we are to know is that God is sovereign and
that His will and purpose stand behind everything that happens. This fact is
independent of our full understanding.

Isaiah prophesied that the LORD would use Cyrus as an instrument to
fulfill His purposes for His people, Israel. A century and a half later He did
that very thing when He used the Persian king to lead the overthrow of the
Babylonians. This allowed the Hebrew people to return home from captivity.
Prior to fulfilling this prophesy, Israel (Judah) had suffered utter destruction
at the hands of the Babylonians. The temple had been destroyed and the city
left in ruin. Yet none of it was outside God's plans and purposes. What kind
of God would allow that to happen? The same questions are asked today
whenever tragedy of whatever magnitude strikes: the death of an infant, a
devastating hurricane, buildings being destroyed, planes crashing—each of
these cases causing innocent lives to be taken. God doesn't mind the question
as to why things such as these happen. Though our understanding will always
be imperfect, and God is pleased when we seek from the heart to understand
His ways. In this very verse, through the prophet Isaiah, God makes it clear
He creates and controls everything, even calamity. Other verses of Scriptures

testify to this fact as well: "Is it not from the mouth of the Most High that both good and bad come?" (Lamentations 3:38), and "Does disaster come to a city, unless the LORD has done it?" (Amos 3:6).

I once heard a prominent pastor comment that there are some who say, in an attempt to get God off the hook for the evil that occurs, He isn't in control of it. Scripture testifies to the contrary. Though God is never responsible for evil, He does allow it to occur. This pastor concluded by saying God doesn't need anyone to take charge of His "public relations" because His Word makes crystal clear exactly who He is. Why is it that we think we can define God outside of the definition He has given us in His Word?

More than asking "why" all the time, perhaps we should try a little harder to understand Him. To understand God is to understand and believe in His sovereignty over everything. This includes the things we like and dislike, want and don't want, understand and don't understand.

A. W. Tozer once wrote, "When we begin to speak of God as having limits; that of which we speak is no longer God." Our God is limitless. Accepting Him for who He says is imperative. He alone defines the terms in which we are to understand Him. Our God is above us in every way. He sees the beginning and the end. He is good, and His purposes are perfect. Be thankful we have a God like that. "For who has known the mind of the Lord, or who has been His counselor?" (Romans 11:34).

Prayer

Father, I thank You that You are a Sovereign God. Forgive me when I don't act as if You are and help me accept the things that seem contrary to who I make You out to be. Your ways are always beyond mine and Your purposes are always good. That includes bringing good out of calamity. Let me submit to Your Word each day that I would see You as You are. Amen!

Monday: Isaiah 44:24-45:7
Tuesday: Isaiah 45:8-25
Wednesday: Amos 3:1-15
Thursday: Lamentations 3:25-39
Friday: Psalm 71:1-24

Week 51

It's Not Who I am, It Is I AM

Who am I that I should go?
—Exodus 3:11

"Who am I that I should go …" (Exodus 3:11) Good question, Moses. Have you ever been really excited about an upcoming role with increasing responsibilities? Maybe a job possibility that sounded great—that is, until you got more information. I believe Moses may have felt the same way. When God called to him from the burning bush, Moses responded, "Here I am" (Exodus 3:4). Moses knew of all the trouble the Egyptians had caused the people of Israel. Though born a Hebrew, Moses spent forty years being raised by Pharaoh's daughter before aligning himself with his own people—in fact killing an Egyptian he saw beating a Hebrew man. The next day Moses saw two Hebrew men struggling with one another, but when he tried to intervene, one said, "Who made you a prince and a judge over us? Do you mean to kill me as you killed the Egyptian?" That sent Moses to the next forty-year period of his life, dwelling in the land of Midian.

At the burning bush, the LORD told Moses He knew of the afflictions of his people and He had come to deliver them out of the hand of the Egyptians. Moses appeared ready to help—that is until the LORD said, "I will send you" (Exodus 3:10). The LORD's intention was for Moses to lead the Israelites out of Egypt and into the Promised Land. Seemingly ready and willing to serve, it was only when the LORD told him of his role that Moses hesitated. He responded with several excuses that came in the form of questions: "Who am I …?" (Exodus 3:11) and "Who are you?" (Exodus 3:13). To the first question, as to who Moses was, was really not the issue. He just happened to be the person the LORD ordained for this purpose. What was important was that the LORD would be with him. That promise and His answer to Moses' second question was not only the key for Moses but for each of us as we serve our LORD as well. When Moses asked "Who are you?" the LORD answered, "I AM WHO I AM" (Exodus 3:14), "YAHWEH," which means He is the eternal, self-existent, self-sufficient, personal, unchanging, and all-powerful God. That really is the only answer any of us will ever need for whatever God may call us to. It's that we have Him with us that matters.

Moses' calling was unique in salvation history. Though our calling may not be as great, it is unique as well and whatever it may be, it will be God's power and promise that it will be fulfilled. Moses was a great leader. He had tremendous humility, faith, and a submissive spirit toward the will of God. Scripture testifies that he was unrivaled among the prophets in Israel's history (Deuteronomy 34:10). But like each of us, Moses was human, who in every way needed a provider and sustainer to accomplish what he was called to do. We need a provider and sustainer for our calling as well. We have that in the LORD. Through ups and downs, Moses was obedient to his calling. Will you be obedient to yours? Let him serve as an example of faithfulness each day. After all, we serve the great "I AM."

Prayer

LORD, thank You for the example of Moses. Thank You that
it was Your sovereignty that allowed him to fulfill the purpose for which
You called him. Help me have the faith to be obedient to Your call on my
life. No matter how big or small that calling is,
I know You will be with me. And I know that is more than enough. Thank
You for daily grace. Amen.

Monday: Exodus 1:1-22
Tuesday: Exodus 2:1-25
Wednesday: Exodus 3:1-22
Thursday: Exodus 4:1-17; Deuteronomy 34:1-12
Friday: Hebrews 11:23-30

Week 52

Reflecting on a Faithful God

But this I call to mind, and therefore I have hope: the steadfast love of the LORD never ceases, his mercies never come to an end; they are new every morning; great is your faithfulness.
—Lamentations 3:21-23

I grew up in North Carolina, where I attended church as a youngster and was involved in the youth group. That changed during my teenage and early adult years as church attendance was almost nonexistent. At any point though, if asked, I would have claimed to be a Christian. I would have claimed it even during the years when I committed my most despicable sins—not that they're not all despicable before a holy God. It was an easy claim to make, but I knew I didn't have any concern for the things of God. Claiming to be a Christian just made me feel better.

Those were good years, or so I thought. It was not until my wife, Karen, became pregnant with Kristin in 1993 that I felt God's prompting of the need to get back into church. I knew the importance of raising my child in church, but I also knew that if Kristin was to be baptized, we needed a church home. As I look back, I realize how gracious God was and how He worked His will even through my misplaced motivation. The quest for a church home, more centered on having Kristin baptized than on seeking God, ended up being the point in which, after a long absence, I was once again exposed to God's Word.

Then in 1996 we moved to Hoover, Alabama. After some delay, I continued to grow in His Word, both through church and for the first time in my life, a men's Bible study. It was during this time that I came to saving faith in Jesus Christ. Some can, but I cannot pinpoint the exact moment God saved me. More importantly, I know He has. What I can pinpoint are the various circumstances and moments in my life that God has used to call me to a deeper walk with Him. I have stumbled many times during that walk.

"But I call this to mind, and therefore have hope: The steadfast love of the LORD never ceases, his mercies never come to an end; they are new every morning; great is your faithfulness" (Lamentations 3:21-23) How many times had the people of Israel promised obedience to the LORD yet broken their covenant with Him? They broke it over and over and over. So have we. Though Jeremiah preached some hard truths about the deserved judgment Israel faced because of their unfaithfulness, he also looked forward with hope to the day Jerusalem would be restored.

In his Bible Handbook, John MacArthur chose the theme "Hope in the Devastation" for the book of Lamentations. If you've brought devastation to your life, you have hope today in the person of Jesus Christ. Maybe you're like I was, claiming to be a Christian, but having no concern for the things of God. God says, "Come to me." Perhaps you are a believer, yet there is no joy in your salvation. Is your Christian life stagnant, with no growth at all? Is your faith always wavering? Are you struggling with sin and disobedience? If so, God has a word for you as well: "Trust me. Trust in my promises. I've given you my Son. Draw on my mercy, draw on my grace, because I love you and that love will never end."

I mentioned that in the years before I was saved how I thought those were the good years. I was deceived. I will say that in those years I never faced some of the difficult periods that have come since becoming a Christian. And though these times weren't and never are easy, the Lord has been faithful. He will be for you as well.

So my testimony is that when I was unlovable, before I knew Jesus as my Savior and Lord, He knew me, and He loved me enough to save me. And though I know Him now as Savior and Lord, I can still be pretty unlovable, but He loves me anyway. That's how our God is, forever gracious and forever faithful. We have a great God who offers us the only hope we have. That hope is in the person of Jesus Christ. We have a great God, who, when you and I are faithless, we can always be thankful that He is not. "Great is your faithfulness"!

Prayer

Father, I have so much to be thankful for. I can't express deeply enough my thankfulness to You for sending Your Son to wash away my sin. Thank You for setting Your love on me. You are a faithful and patient God. Keep me close, Lord, that I may do Your will. Give me the grace to live each day to Your glory. Amen!

Monday: Jeremiah 1:1-19; Lamentations 3:1-24
Tuesday: Jeremiah 30:1-31:40
Wednesday: Jeremiah 32:1-33:26; Exodus 34: 6-7; Micah 7:18-20
Thursday: Psalm 42:1-11, 108:1-4
Friday: 1 Thessalonians 5:23-24; 2 Timothy 2:13; Hebrews 10:19-23